WITH FRIENDS LIKE YOU

THE FREE PRESS

A Division of Macmillan, Inc.
NEW YORK

Maxwell Macmillan Canada
TORONTO

Maxwell Macmillan International
NEW YORK OXFORD SINGAPORE SYDNEY

WITH FRIENDS LIKE YOU

What Israelis Really Think
About American Jews

MATTI GOLAN

Translated from the Hebrew by
HILLEL HALKIN

The Free Press
A Division of Macmillan, Inc.
866 Third Avenue, New York, N.Y. 10022

Maxwell Macmillan Canada, Inc.
1200 Eglinton Avenue East
Suite 200
Don Mills, Ontario M3C 3N1

Macmillan, Inc. is part of the Maxwell Communication Group of Companies.

Printed in the United States of America

printing number

1   2   3   4   5   6   7   8   9   10

Library of Congress Cataloging-in-Publication Data

Golan, Matti.
   With friends like you : what Israelis really think about American Jews /
by Matti Golan ; translated from the Hebrew by Hillel Halkin.
      p.   cm.
   ISBN 0-02-912064-0
   1. Jews—United States—Public opinion.   2. Public opinion—
Israel.   3. Jews—United States—Attitudes toward Israel.   4. Public
opinion—United States.   5. Israel and the diaspora.   6. Israel—
Foreign public opinion, American.   7. United States—Foreign public
opinion, Israeli.   8. Imaginary conversations.   I. Title.
E184.J5G594   1992
305.892'4073—dc20   92-22615
                                                                      CIP

To Nili
my wife and my love

Contents

Prologue

"As I see it," I said to Elie Wiesel, "you're a worse enemy of mine and of Israel than Yasser Arafat."

We were sitting in the lobby of the King David Hotel. It was late afternoon, and through the picture windows we could see the waning light glinting off the walls of the old city of Jerusalem. All around us was the usual bustle of American tourists, senior government and Jewish Agency officials, and Arab waiters.

Wiesel's face, so suited to the professional Holocaust survivor he has chosen to be, had its usual tormented look: its cheekbones prominent, its nose aquiline, its eyes candescent above his small, thin body. "When you say 'you,'" he asked, "do you mean me personally?"

"I mean the Jews of the United States *and* you personally, both because in no small measure you have become the symbol of those Jews and because as their intellectual spokesman you legitimize the harm they do to Israel."

"What harm is that?"

"Paving the way for its demise. If things continue as they are, that demise is a foregone conclusion. And its main cause will have been not the deeds and misdeeds of the PLO, but, to a large extent, those of American Jewry."

Wiesel stared silently into space. In that silence I added: "Not that American Jews will escape the same fate, caused by the same deeds and misdeeds."

Wiesel continued to focus on some indefinite point in the lobby of the hotel, which once, several decades ago, had been the military headquarters of the British Mandate in Palestine. I could all but hear the wheels turning in his head: Was the conversation worth continuing? At last he said: "Such a harsh accusation calls for an explanation."

We talked for more than two hours. Actually, it was I who did most of the talking. This book is an expatiation on that conversation. And since the problem was not a personal one, I wrote about it in the form of a dialogue between an Israeli and an American Jew, each more or less representing the mainstream of thought in his community. While the Israeli's statements represent my own opinions, those of the American Jew are certainly not meant to represent the opinions of Elie Wiesel. The work attempts to dramatize ideas and sentiments that are held on both sides, but expressed by no particular individual.

This dialogue is not symmetrical. The American Jew is a largely passive participant who listens more than he speaks his own mind. When he does say or ask something, it is to enable the Israeli to express his opinions on American Jewry—opinions that few Israelis make public for reasons that form part of the contents of this book.

1

Who Is the Enemy?

AMERICAN JEW: Hello.

ISRAELI JEW: Shalom.

AMERICAN: You wanted to meet with me?

ISRAELI: Yes. Thank you for finding the time.

AMERICAN: You said it was urgent. What is it? What's it about?

ISRAELI: It seems from all I've heard and read that you have a lot of grievances against me.

AMERICAN: What are you talking about?

ISRAELI: Your American newspapers are full of reports that you don't like what I'm doing.

AMERICAN: Such as what, for example?

ISRAELI: Such as my behavior in the occupied territories.

AMERICAN: And you *do* like what you're doing there?

ISRAELI: You especially don't like the settlements, because you think they're detrimental to the peace process.

AMERICAN: Don't you?

ISRAELI: I'm told also you're unhappy with the political chaos in Israel, and with the role of the rabbinical establishment in national policy decisions.

AMERICAN: Aren't you unhappy with it too? Is any of my criticism wide of the mark?

ISRAELI: That isn't relevant.

AMERICAN: Then what is?

ISRAELI: The only relevant question is who is responsible for the situation. Before we can even hope to solve the problems you're pointing to, we have to know the answer to that.

3

AMERICAN: What do you mean, who is responsible? Whoever caused them is responsible.

ISRAELI: And you think the honor is mine.

AMERICAN: Who else's?

ISRAELI: I think it's yours.

AMERICAN: What? How can I be responsible for your behavior?

ISRAELI: Your question just proves how important it is that you listen to what I think about you—to all of it. Are you ready to do that?

AMERICAN: Of course. I'm always ready to listen to you.

ISRAELI: I can see that I've lost you before I've even begun.

AMERICAN: Heavens, no! What gave you that idea?

ISRAELI: Two things. The first is that if you cared, you would have asked me why it was important. You would have been curious instead of saying you're happy to talk with me the same way people say "Let's get together some time" without bothering to take out their appointment book.

AMERICAN: And the second thing?

ISRAELI: The yawn that you didn't quite manage to stifle.

AMERICAN: I'm sorry I gave you that impression. I assure you that I really am interested. Why don't you tell me why it's important.

ISRAELI: It's important because you haven't a clue.

AMERICAN: A clue to what?

ISRAELI: To what I think of you.

AMERICAN: No offense meant, but just who are you?

ISRAELI: A very good question. Before we begin, let's get our identities straight. The basic ground rule should be that each of us represents a real element in the community he's speaking for. Who goes first?

AMERICAN: This conversation was your idea—I think I deserve to know who you are.

ISRAELI: Gladly. I suggest that I be a native-born Israeli in his late forties, the son of parents who immigrated to Israel, or Palestine, as it was called at the time, sometime in the 1930s.

AMERICAN: Before the Holocaust?

ISRAELI: Yes. And for authenticity's sake, let's also say I'm a journalist who has spent a good deal of time working in your country. I'm comfortably off but not rich and live in a well-to-do suburb of Tel Aviv. Have I left anything out?

AMERICAN: Do you have children?

ISRAELI: I have two: a son in the army—an officer in a combat unit—and a daughter finishing high school.

AMERICAN: Pleased to meet you. And who am I.

ISRAELI: If you have no objection, I'd say you're pretty much the same.

AMERICAN: Meaning?

ISRAELI: That you're a native-born American of about fifty.

AMERICAN: In my late forties!

ISRAELI: Okay. Your parents fled Eastern Europe in the 1930s, too, but unlike mine, they went to America. You have two children also. Your daughter is finishing high school like mine. But your son—ah, here there's a difference. It's one we'll get around to. He's the same age as my son, but he's not in any army. He's a college student, just like you once were. And you're a professional like me, although—but this is a difference you won't regret— you make a lot more money than I do. Have I left anything out?

AMERICAN: I need to live somewhere.

ISRAELI: Of course you do. How about a somewhat or a more-than-somewhat affluent suburb in a more-than-somewhat middle-sized city? Is that typical enough for you?

AMERICAN: But why should you want to tell a somewhat typical Jew like myself what you think of him?

ISRAELI: Because it's Jews like you who are the heart of the problem. You're someone with what's known as "a deep personal commitment to Israel." You do all the right things. You give to the United Jewish Appeal. You visit Israel every couple of years and never forget to bring back a souvenir from the Wailing Wall and a painting from the artists' colony in Safed. You're a member of the board of your Reform synagogue. You attend every meeting, every dinner, and every brunch, not a few of which you host in your own house. You listen with unfailing politeness to the dozens of speakers who come to your community from Israel to tell you for the umpteenth time what you already know by heart. Right now you're the local president of the

UJA, having been Jewish National Fund chairman last year. Next year you'll be chairman of the bonds drive, and the year after that the head of the local American Jewish Congress chapter. You are, without a doubt, the salt of the American Jewish earth. Am I right about that?

AMERICAN: It sounds familiar enough.

ISRAELI: In a word, you're the man to whom my leaders, spokesmen, and emissaries come to tell what you want to hear.

AMERICAN: How about giving us names?

ISRAELI: Good point. "The American," "the Israeli"—how tiresome! I'm open to suggestions.

AMERICAN: Well now, let's see. I think I have just the name for you. Israel—how's that?

ISRAELI: Yes, that will do. It's certainly Israeli enough. But how about you?

AMERICAN: Steven, Harry, Frank—take your pick. They're all distinguishedly average.

ISRAEL: What we need, I think, is a name that says Jew the minute you hear it.

AMERICAN: By "you," you mean a non-Jew, I suppose.

ISRAEL: I've got it! How obvious. Judah! The other part of the ancient Jewish kingdom. It's perfect.

AMERICAN: Judah? You think it's representative? I don't know anyone called that.

ISRAEL: Maybe you know someone whose middle name it is? The one he never uses?

7

JUDAH: It's possible.

ISRAEL: Excellent. Now that we both know whom we're talking to, we can get on with our conversation.

JUDAH: I must confess that I'm still not sure what you have in mind. Actually, it's my impression that we converse all the time. You're often in America. I'm here in Israel even more. We have joint conferences, congresses, seminars, study groups, rallies, formal dinners—a complete industry of dialogue that's hard at work on our relationship day and night. What could you possibly tell me that I haven't already heard?

ISRAEL: The truth.

JUDAH: What have you been telling me until now?

ISRAEL: What you've wanted to hear.

JUDAH: But why start telling me the truth now?

ISRAEL: Because you're the largest and most important part of the people we both belong to. I couldn't exist without you, nor perhaps could you without me. And I believe that that existence—yours as a Jew and mine as an Israeli—is in danger. That's what makes it crucial to speak frankly.

JUDAH: I'm sorry, but I don't share your doomsday views.

ISRAEL: I'm talking about facts, not opinions. I'm talking about 500,000 people who have left Israel since its establishment. I am talking about more than 20,000 *yordim** every year, 10 percent of whom are scientists, doctors, engineers, computer experts, and other technological professionals.

---

* In Hebrew "those who go down," the term used for Jews emigrating from Israel.

8

There are very few fields in which we can successfully compete with other countries. If only they would recognize *yerida** as a competitive branch in the Olympic Games, we would at long last win a medal. According to a Gallup poll conducted for the *Ha'aretz* newspaper in 1990, the desire of Israelis to emigrate from their country even exceeded that of the East Europeans. Only Czechoslovakia beat us in this area. But let's not despair. If we accept the figures of Mordechai Lipman, secretary-general of the Council to Combat Yerida (there are already at least two such organizations), we will soon catch up and take first place. The forecast is that by the year 2000, more than 800,000 Israelis will have left the country, about 15 percent of the present population.

And no one is ashamed anymore about leaving the country. Fifteen or twenty years ago, even the thought of leaving almost amounted to betrayal. If I had been planning such a step, I would have kept it a secret, and disappeared without saying good-bye to my friends. Now it's almost legitimate. A telling sign of this fact was the way Yitzhak Rabin, leader of the Labor party, reacted to the subject. When he was prime minister (1974–77), during one of his visits to the United States, Rabin called the *yordim* "the dregs of Israeli society". Needless to say, this aroused an enormous furor—protests, demands for an apology, even demonstrations. But Rabin stubbornly stuck to his opinion. Not for long though. At the beginning of April 1991, he gave an interview to the *yordim* newspaper *Los Angeles News,* in which he stated, "What I said then

* The Hebrew word for "descent," used to refer to the emigration of Jews from Israel.

doesn't apply today." And he explained, "The Israelis living abroad are an integral part of the Jewish community and there is no point in talking about ostracism." Ted Arenson, a billionaire and himself an ex-Israeli who left in the fifties, concurred with that sentiment. At a meeting of *yordim* held in Miami at the end of May 1991, he brought his audience a momentous message. There was no need for them to feel ashamed about leaving Israel; rather the state of Israel ought to be ashamed for causing its young people to leave. "The Government made Israel into too small a place for a lot of Israelis," he informed his listeners. And who was in the audience? Israel's deputy foreign minister, Benyamin Netanyahu, and the consul-general of Miami, Moshe Liba.

Moreover, this attitude is not only legitimate today, almost normative, but rather it's a cause for envy, if not outright admiration. Friends and relatives all want to know how you did it, how you found a job, how much you will make, how you got a work permit, and they urge the *yored* to let them know if he finds a job for them. One of the most popular topics in the supplements of the weekend newspapers are success stories about Israelis in America.

JUDAH: Most of them don't make it.

ISRAEL: You're talking about money, but you can't seem to understand that it's not only that. The very fact that they're in America and not in Israel is considered a success. Because in America they're not called to reserve duty, their children don't have to serve in the army, they don't have to give half of their earnings to income tax, their daily routine doesn't include the PLO, settlements, and other existential problems. That's why there aren't many Israelis who

10

wouldn't pack their bags and leave their homeland if they got a reasonable job offer. Our children serve in combat units and then take off for New York or Los Angeles. They would rather move furniture in New Jersey than live in Israel. Thousands of our best brains end up in Silicon Valley. Tens of thousands of doctors, scientists, engineers, the cream of our young people leave because they've had enough and don't know why they should bear the burden any longer. A U.S. green card has become the new Zionist dream of the average Israeli.

JUDAH: That's a pretty shocking admission. I always thought that you Israelis were the most passionate of patriots.

ISRAEL: We are. But we're tired. We can't carry the burden any longer by ourselves. We're not willing to carry it any longer by ourselves.

JUDAH: But you're not carrying it by yourselves! We're helping you as best we can. We consider ourselves full partners in the enterprise of Israel.

ISRAEL: That's just an empty UJA cliché.

JUDAH: I'm sorry, but I believe it to be true.

ISRAEL: That's why it's so important for you to listen to me, because of all the crap in our relationship, this partner business is the worst!

JUDAH: I'd appreciate your not shouting.

ISRAEL: Why? Let's talk for once like human beings instead of diplomats! Let's cut out all the "I'm sorry"s and the "I'm afraid that"s and "I'd appreciate"s. The issues are too important to softsoap. Let's shout, let's lose our

11

tempers, let's be emotional. I want to tell you what I really think about you in the realest way I can.

JUDAH: Just a minute, Izzy . . .

ISRAEL: I'd rather you didn't call me that.

JUDAH: Why not?

ISRAEL: Because only my friends do and you're not one of them.

JUDAH: I'm not your friend, I'm not your partner—what exactly am I?

ISRAEL: In more ways than one, you're my enemy. A more harmful and dangerous one than the PLO. Where are you going?

JUDAH: I don't have to sit here and listen to this. How can I be a worse enemy than the organization that's out to destroy you? Tell me how!

ISRAEL: It's time you listened to the truth, even if you don't find it flattering.

JUDAH: Worse than the PLO? That's what you call the truth?

ISRAEL: In the long run, it's not always the terrorists who cause the worst damage. I can always take countermeasures against them, especially when I know what they're up to. And that's the case with the PLO. The Palestinians think I stole their homeland. They want it back. They say they're my enemy and I'm theirs. I know where I stand with them and what I have to do to stop them. They tell me the truth, not a lot of tall tales. Whereas you say you're my friend, that you support me, that you love me. But your actual record, which I'll get around to shortly, is enormously

12

harmful to me. The PLO could never harm me as much, and what harm it does is also your doing.

JUDAH: My doing? Are you crazy? I'm the man who gives you money, who provides you with the political support of the United States, who has been your partner since the day you came into existence

ISRAEL: What kind of partnership are you talking about? How can there be a partnership between someone who sends his son to fight in Lebanon or the Occupied Territories and someone who sends his son to college? Between someone who spends three whole years of his life in the Israeli army, plus an annual month of reserve duty until middle age, and someone who comes as a tourist to Israel now and then? Between someone who pays over 50 percent of his income in taxes to the Israeli government and someone who contributes barely 1 percent of his—and even that, in many cases, because it's partly tax deductible!

JUDAH: But what's wrong with that? Why can't I be your junior partner?

ISRAEL: Because every partnership, full or partial, is based on a balance of privileges and obligations. What you're asking for are the privileges of a senior partner and the obligations of a less than junior one.

JUDAH: I do the best I can.

ISRAEL: You still can't stop mouthing slogans, can you? At most you do what you can within the limits of what you think you can do. That's a long, long way from your best, or even from you most middling.

JUDAH: What more do you expect of me?

ISRAEL: What more do I expect of you? . . . Hundreds of thousands of Jews come to Israel, penniless, speaking a foreign language, with a fifties mentality, and I'm supposed to provide them with housing and jobs, and at the same time look after all my security concerns. And you ask what more I want from you? Maybe for you it's long forgotten history, but I still hear the shrieks of the sirens calling us to go down to the shelters, sitting there wearing a gas mask, my heart pumping wildly as I wait to hear the sound of the Scud missile exploding so I'll know it fell somewhere else. And you ask what more I want from you? Nearly every day I accompany people, young and old, men, women and children, to their graves after being shot or stabbed. And you ask what more I want from you? And while all of this is going on, I have to fight with your government about every step that I take, when your only worry is how to get out of this conflict unscathed. And that's why—and not because you have my good in mind—that's why you criticize me, interfere in my affairs, and tell me what I should do. It's not out of concern for me, but concern for your own skin. And you ask what more I want from you?

But since you ask, I'll tell you. What I want from you is to enable me to absorb the hundreds of thousands of immigrants without having to see hungry people sleeping in parks or in doorways. What I want from you is that after so many years I should be able to sit in my own home in security and tranquillity. What I want from you is that my economy be sound. What I want from you is that I shouldn't have to fight with your government. What I want from you is that my son shouldn't have to fight in any wars.

You are my brother. By blood. But as long as you don't give me all these things, you're not my friend. You're not my partner. You are my enemy. My enemy brother.

JUDAH: I can understand—not agree, but understand—when you say I am not a friend and not a partner. But an enemy? To be an enemy I have to do something that causes you harm, that hurts you. What is that something that makes me an enemy in your eyes?

ISRAEL: The vicious circle.

JUDAH: What vicious circle?

ISRAEL: The circle in which the Jews in Israel leave their homeland and the Jews in America leave their Judaism; the circle in which nearly all the things that happen to me, all that you blame me for, is really the result of your actions or inactions.

JUDAH: That's a new one!

ISRAEL: No, it isn't. It's just something that no one ever talks about.

JUDAH: Why not?

ISRAEL: Because those who could and should talk about it—both on your side and on mine—don't want to. They like things too much the way they are. And it's this conspiracy of silence and deceit that permits the vicious circle to exist.

JUDAH: Would you mind being more specific?

ISRAEL: Would I mind? I've been waiting for this chance for years! Where should I begin?

JUDAH: Wherever you like. I'm here mostly to listen, isn't that what you said?

15

~~~~~~~~

ISRAEL: All right, then. I think the best place to start is with feelings. With our emotional identities, as it were. Because sitting here and looking at you—at everything you stand for—I feel that we not only aren't partners, we don't even share the closeness of belonging to the same people. I feel you're a stranger to me, like a distant relative you only meet at funerals and weddings, so that each time you meet him you discover all over that the two of you have nothing in common.

JUDAH: Abraham, Moses, the Wailing Wall, anti-Semitism. Aren't those things we have in common?

ISRAEL: That's on the collective Jewish level. But the truth is that we have very different emotional identities due to my having been born and raised as a member of a majority and you as a member of a minority.

JUDAH: How does that make us different?

ISRAEL: It's a difference I only became aware of the first time I left Israel. I had never been abroad before. My father had just died. He was forty-four, an age at which the first heart attack is often the last. I was nearly twenty-one and had just finished my stint in the army. I didn't have a particularly glorious career there. Rigid structures never brought out the best in me, and the more rigid they were, the worse I functioned in them.

It's a big shock to lose your father at such a young age. Your whole life changes. Instead of a mother, you're suddenly faced with a widow. Instead of a younger sister, with an orphan. Instead of a warm, indulgent home, with one that's dreary and depressing.

Anyway, some two months after my father's death I received a letter from his brother, my uncle who lived in Australia, inviting me to stay with him and study at the university there. I didn't think twice. It was an excellent way to get away from home with its oppressive daily reminders of loss.

From the start Melbourne seemed to me a distinctly unmemorable city, a flat, functional, formless sort of place. My aunt and uncle came to meet me at the airport. They were in their middle forties and had three sons. The minute they brought me home with them I realized that I had been adopted by an unusual species of Jews, both in general and in Australia in particular. I was indeed the rare Jew with relatives in Australia who were not rolling in money.

Believe me, Judah, it was an awkward situation. None of my friends in Israel believed me. They were all certain it was just a story to keep them from coming to scrounge off me, or something like that. To be Jewish and Australian, no less than Jewish and American, seemed to them—and to me—as sure a formula for wealth as one plus one equals two.

It was just my luck, though, that one plus one equaled three. Did I say three? Nine! The family lived in a little, old two-story house in remote and rundown suburb. Once, during the mass immigration from Europe after World War II, it had been a Jewish neighborhood, but most of the Jews had long moved to newer and more expensive areas and made way for Chinese, Indians, and

Pakistanis. Well, that's something you're familiar with better than I am.

In the front of the first floor my aunt and uncle had what was called a "milk shop," which was a sort of halfway house between a grocery and a cafe. People came to buy soft drinks, candy, ice cream, milk shakes, nuts, as well as ordinary groceries. In the back was a guest room, but since there were never any guests—who had time for them?—it served as a family room. Next to it was the kitchen, which was the nerve center of the house. Overhead, on the second floor, were the bedrooms. I shared one of them with my cousin, the eldest of the three brothers.

I can hardly remember my aunt and uncle ever resting. The shop was open from 6:00 A.M. till midnight, seven days a week. Now and then one of them would step into the living room, only to hurry back into the shop when the bell announced a customer. Still, it all added up. It added up to a great deal. Because no matter how few Australian pounds they made or how many thousands and millions they didn't make, their hearts and souls were worth a fortune. From the day I arrived I was one of the family. There was no standing on ceremony with me and no empty gestures. In the natural and unassuming manner of simple people they made me feel that I had been taken into their hearts as well as into their home. I didn't feel that I was their son—I *was* their son.

I especially remember the evenings, when the whole family would sit down for supper—or, as they called it for arcane reasons, "tea"—around a little old kitchen table that was always sparkling clean and full of warmth and good smells. Afterwards, my two bigger cousins would go off somewhere, leaving me with the youngest of the three, a boy of six, to watch what for an Israeli like me had until then been only a rumored wonder: television. During my first weeks there I couldn't be budged from the set. Every half-hour or so my aunt or uncle would come running in from the store with another snack—peanuts, chocolate, ice cream, or a big, thick milkshake in a glass.

I received my first lesson in the difference between us—between you and me—the day after arriving in Melbourne. In my honor we went out to eat. All the while that we were reading the menu, ordering, and chatting while waiting for the food, my uncle sat facing the door and announcing whether each new arrival was a Jew or a Gentile. I could tell from his voice that he felt better when the newcomer was a Jew. One more of "us"! What I couldn't understand was how he recognized them. My uncle, for his part, couldn't understand my question. "What do you mean, how? Everyone can see it. Can't you?"

"No."

"But it's obvious!"

"It's not obvious to me. What's so special about the Jews?"

"What do you mean, what's so special? What's so special is that they don't look like goyim. Here, look at that man coming in now. It's clear as day. You couldn't possibly mistake him."

"For a goy?"

"What are you talking about? Can't you see he *is* a goy?"

I couldn't and I still don't. Because it's not on my mind.

19

Because when you belong to a majority you don't need to know who's who and to be always on the lookout for allies. You don't have the anxieties and the lack of confidence that a member of a minority does, especially of a minority that's been persecuted like we have been. That's why I don't see Jews or non-Jews, I only see human beings. They may be black human beings, or white human beings, or slanty-eyed human beings, but human beings is all they are for me. And among the white, round-eyed human beings I can't tell the Jews from the non-Jews anymore than I can tell the Christians from the Buddhists among the slanty eyes. It's not just a matter of how I see, it's a matter of how I think, too. And the same holds true for you.

JUDAH: I live surrounded by Gentiles. You live surrounded by Arabs. I'll bet you can recognize them.

ISRAEL: It's not the same thing. I may be surrounded by hostile people, but I'm still the majority in my own country.

Today I realize that back then, in that restaurant, I didn't just get my first glimpse of how you and I are strangers to each other. I also got my first inkling of what Zionism means in a personal rather than a national sense. I'm talking about the importance of Israel not as a Jewish home, but as a *home,* period. The difference between our two mentalities is the difference between someone who lives at home and someone who lives in a rented room. The family you rent from may be the kindest and nicest you could wish for, but you still have to behave yourself and stay in its good graces if you don't want to be out of a room.

You know who else is aware of this difference? The non-Jews. Already in Australia I noticed that non-Jews related to Israelis differently from how they did to Jews. This was brought home to me more concretely in Canada, though, when I was traveling by train from Montreal to Ottawa some twenty years ago. I had stepped into the dining car to have some supper and had been seated by the waiter in the only available space, opposite a passenger who was already eating. He must have been in his fifties, an elegantly dressed man with silvery hair who turned out to be the owner and director of a fairly large business concern. He was a cultured person and a pleasant conversation partner who asked many questions about Israel, about life there, and about our wars. He was eager to visit there, he told me, in order to see the Christian holy places. Eventually, the conversation shifted to Canada. And then to the Jews. Perfectly naturally, without the slightest hint of embarrassment, he observed that most of them were involved in finance, the clear implication being that he thought you all shylocks. I don't remember the details, but the bottom line was that he did not have a particularly high opinion of you. I began to feel a bit uncomfortable.

JUDAH: That's all? *A bit* uncomfortable?

ISRAEL: I wasn't sure I understood him. I told him that though he might not be aware of it, most Israelis, including myself, were Jews, too. How could I think that he wasn't aware of it, he replied. Of course he was! "But it's not the same thing," he explained straightforwardly. "You Israelis aren't like Jews at all." When I asked him what the

21

difference was, he thought for a moment and answered, "That's obvious. You have a home."

JUDAH: Which made you feel good.

ISRAEL: Perhaps it did a bit.

JUDAH: Well, I have news for you. Your dinner partner was an ordinary anti-Semite.

ISRAEL: Then so am I. Because I notice the same difference he did. And shall I tell you something? So do you. That's why you don't like me anymore than I like you.

JUDAH: I rather think that I like you considerably more than you like me.

ISRAEL: Come, come: Why don't you tell the truth? I get on your nerves. Honestly, isn't that what you say about me when you're alone with your friends? That I'm arrogant? Aggressive? Loud-mouthed? You don't exactly consider me the type you'd like to spend a vacation with or have as a long-term house guest, do you?

JUDAH: I don't deny that we differ in mentality, in behavior, in thought processes. That's pretty obvious. But it doesn't keep me from admiring you and even, yes, from feeling a deep affection for you.

ISRAEL: I think you're using words too loosely. What you feel for me is the special connection of belonging to the same people. But there's a catch here, too. Do you know why? Because your feeling of affection depends almost entirely on what I can do for your own self-image. That's why you had genuinely warm feelings for me when I triumphed over the combined armies of half-a-dozen Arab countries in my War of Independence. I was the good little

David vanquishing the big bad Goliath against all odds and expectations. And in doing so, I made you a state.

JUDAH: You made *me* a state? Somehow I thought you made it for yourself.

ISRAEL: Of course I did. But the country I fought for was for you, too, even if you didn't fight. It was my struggle, yet it changed you from a homeless minority to a minority with a country. I gave you something to make you feel proud of. I was a hero, although still a pretty ragged-looking one, poor, hungry, and dressed in tatters—the beloved but less fortunate cousin who gets sent care packages and old clothes. It was only in 1967 that, with one swift blow, I lost my pitiable look. In six days I defeated three Arab armies and overran territories twice my own size.

JUDAH: I'm glad you mentioned the Six Day War. I'll never forget the days before it. President Nasser of Egypt had blockaded the Straits of Tiran. The Egyptian, Syrian, and Jordanian armies were massed along your borders, surrounding you on all sides. I remember dropping everything to sit glued to the radio and television around the clock. And to pray. Nonstop. With tears in my eyes. And to pray some more. Physically I was in America, but my heart was with you.

ISRAEL: Yes. That's precisely the point, isn't it? I can tell you quite categorically that your heart helped me very little in those days. I was staring destruction in the face. I—you— the whole world—saw it as more than just a possibility; it seemed almost a certainty. And what did you do about it? You cried and prayed and sent me your heart. But your body stayed in America. Do you know what would have happened if all the predictions had come true? You would have cried and prayed for my soul a little harder, but you would have gone on living while I would have been dead.

Luckily, I won the war. And what a victory it was! You were beside yourself with love and admiration. Now—Leon Uris had been twenty years before his time—I became for you and the world the sun-bronzed, handsome, rugged, fearless Ari ben Canaan. All your life you had been hearing from non-Jews how unattractive you were, how you only cared about money, how you couldn't be counted on, how you were a coward—and now along I came and gave you the chance to answer back: "See, we Jews can fight, too—can even do it better than you can." You also became Ari ben Canaan, although not really. You were the Paul Newman who played the role of Ari ben Canaan, the Jew who changed his name in order to succeed in the world of non-Jews, and made it. The Jew about whom you and your friends say proudly: "He's Jewish, you know." The successful Jew who plays a character that symbolizes all the things he is not—the Jew with the state, the Jew who is in the majority and it doesn't occur to him to say: "He's a Jew, you know." Not that the Gentiles swallowed it completely. They never made, as I have said, the mistake of confusing you with me. But certainly some of me rubbed off on you. You bought yourself some self-esteem, and cheaply at that.

JUDAH: You're forgetting that I paid for it with hundreds of millions of dollars and United States support.

ISRAEL: Excuse me, but a bit of lobbying in Washington and some partly tax-deductible contributions were a small price to pay for the blood I spilled. But let's not get into that now. We'll come back to it later. I really have no complaints about those days. I got a big kick out of seeing myself as you and the world saw me. Being an Israeli was a wonderful thing then. You told me how brave, handsome, and clever I was, and I didn't bother to deny it. I wanted to believe and did believe that I was all those things and that you loved me for myself, unconditionally, the way you love your own child. I believed every word you said about our being one people, about our being brothers, about our being partners. It never occurred to me that what you actually loved was not me but what I had done for you. And if it did, I rejected it immediately. Because to believe that would have meant giving up the conceited notion that I was perhaps not quite as wonderful as the whole world said I was and as I wanted so badly to believe.

Yes, it was wonderful to be an Israeli after 1967. To be brave, clever, and right—and to feel loved. Yes, it was great to be the Israeli who flew to Entebbe and rescued the hostages from right under the evil noses of the terrorists and Ugandan soldiers, and then took his bows to get the applause he so richly deserved from the world. It was like an idyllic dream in which you were surrounded by people who wanted nothing more than to be near you and smile at you. The flowers smelled better than ever, the sky was bluer than ever, the song of the birds had never been so joyous and pure.

That's what made the morning after so awful.

JUDAH: You look like you're going to cry!

ISRAEL: I hadn't realized how painful it is to remember. Perhaps that's because our private egos as Israelis are so closely identified with out national ego. Whatever happens to our country has an immediate effect on our lives. I suppose that's one of the hallmarks of a small society. Or perhaps of one that has never from the moment of its birth been able to give its citizens a feeling of permanence. In any case, the awakening was a rude one.

The sixth of October 1973 was Yom Kippur. I happened to be in London, and I hope you'll forgive me for revealing that I spent the day shopping on Oxford Street. When I returned to my hotel in the early afternoon, I received a phone call from a friend who was also in London. "Have you heard the news?" he asked.

"What news?"

"There's a war on. The Egyptians and the Syrians have attacked Israel."

I thought he was pulling my leg. How could Egypt and Syria have attacked Israel? Didn't they know that I was the wise, brave, handsome Ari ben Canaan? Didn't they know that attacking me was suicidal? They couldn't possibly have dared start up with me! But as soon as I turned on the radio, I found out that they had. Well, there we were: No one had ever accused the Arabs of being too bright. If they wanted a second helping of 1967, we would have no choice but to give it to them.

Being a typical Israeli for those days, I did everything possible to get a seat on an El Al flight to Israel that same day. Later I found out that it was the last civilian flight of its kind for a long time.

Aboard the plane I ran into the familiar all-star Israeli war team: the conductor Zubin Mehta, the ex-Israeli pianist Daniel Barenboim, various senior politicians and officials whom the war had caught unprepared and who couldn't afford not to have it on their curriculum vitae. We were a boisterous, merry crowd of people. The excitement of the war had leveled all barriers and everyone quickly became friends, chatting, telling jokes, and above all, reminiscing about previous wars. When the pilot announced that we were making our approach to Ben-Gurion Airport, it was entirely natural to break into a rousing chorus of "Jerusalem of Gold," the song of that wonderful 1967 war.

And then the doors of the plane opened and we walked down the ramp into a great hush. The jokes, songs, and comradely slaps on the back stopped at once. We couldn't see a thing. The airport was totally blacked out. How come? What was happening? Were we afraid of an enemy air raid? Here, in the middle of Israel, right outside Tel Aviv? What on earth was going on? Hadn't we knocked out the enemy's air forces yet?

For the first time it dawned on me that we had a real war on our hands, not a quick, boisterous victory parade. Still, I found it hard to believe that Arab planes could possibly strike at the heart of Israel. Someone was just taking precautions, which were no doubt unnecessary and exaggerated.

I drove straight from the airport to the headquarters of the army press corps, in which I served as a reservist. In peacetime my reserve duty had generally consisted of escorting groups of foreign journalists to military sites and interviews. In wartime I was supposed to be attached to our frontline forces as a reporter.

Headquarters was full of journalists exchanging information largely based on rumor. It was hard to gauge the mood. The jokes sounded forced a bit, the laughter was brief and hesitant. When I was asked by the mobilization officer whether I preferred being sent up north or down south, I answered that I didn't like the desert and he said, "Okay, I'm assigning you to a paratroop unit that is going to take Mount Hermon tomorrow."

I thought that either he was joking or I hadn't heard right. "What do you mean, take Mount Hermon? Mount Hermon is ours!"

"Was ours. Until this morning."

I heard the rest on the way to the jumping-off point. The Egyptians had crossed the Suez Canal. The Syrians were advancing on the Golan Heights. Our forces were retreating.

Ari ben Canaan was retreating.

We reached the foothills of Mount Hermon late that night: a tent city of soldiers resting, cleaning their weapons, talking quietly. The air was full of tense anticipation.

I was summoned to the commanding officer. In a dry, weary tone of voice he told me that "they caught us with our pants down." The Syrians had taken the mountain on the first day of combat. The fate of the soldiers who had held it was unknown, but no one had great hopes for them. At sunrise, I was told, our counterattack would begin. The original plan had been to use armored vehicles, but then it was decided to switch to helicopters. I would be on the first chopper.

I left the CO's tent, went off to a dark corner, and curled up in the sleeping bag I had been given. I couldn't fall asleep, though. When I opened my eyes all I saw was the huge, imposing silhouette of the mountain. "The eyes of Israel," it had been called, because on its summit was one of the most sophisticated radar and early-warning stations in the world, surrounded by the strongest fortifications in the country. Every child knew that it was the best-defended spot in Israel. And now it had been taken by the enemy. The Arabs had poked out the eyes of Israel.

Even today, when I talk about it, I can still taste the salt of my tears. I let them run down my cheeks, down my neck. I was crying for my country. And for myself. For the two of us, me and it.

It was then, while looking up at Mount Hermon, that I was stuck full force by the brutal and terrible realization that as of the previous morning Israel would never be the same. Nor would I. Neither of us would ever be as handsome, as brave, as clever, and as right as we had been before.

JUDAH: I don't suppose you ever were. Not really.

ISRAEL: What difference does it make? You believed I was, the world believed I was, and I believed I was. That means I was.

JUDAH: But what do you want from me? If you stopped believing in yourself, why should I have continued?

ISRAEL: I thought that at least you would tell me that, in spite of everything, you felt the same about me. Instead you started to distance yourself, to abandon me.

JUDAH: What are you accusing me of? Of abandoning you because your image had changed? That isn't fair and it isn't true. I went on supporting you politically in Washington and I continued sending you my financial support, more even than before.

ISRAEL: There's no need to get excited. If you'll hear me out to the end, perhaps you'll see what I'm getting at. Of course, you're right. Technically speaking, you didn't abandon me. You continued to give me your political support and your dollars. But I was no longer a relative you were proud of and eager to help.

JUDAH: Just what makes you say that?

ISRAEL: The things I've heard you say about me. Those were the years in which you first began to doubt, in fact, to challenge, the centrality of Israel in your life.

JUDAH: You could hear doubts like that in America since the day Israel was established, even before that.

ISRAEL: Certainly. But from explicitly anti-Zionist spokesmen and organizations. After the Yom Kippur War we began hearing such declarations from spokesmen and organizations who, until then, had always accepted the premise of Israel's central place in Jewish life. You may not have said so in so many words, but I could feel that you now thought of me as of a relative who was a nuisance and whom you supported only so as not to stand accused of indifference toward your family—and also, because you still couldn't be certain that you might not need him one day.

Do you follow me? You went on doing the same things as before, but it was now in spite of who I was rather than because of who I was. You clenched your jaws and did it more and more grudgingly.

After the Yom Kippur War came the Arab oil boycott. America had a cold winter. True, it was the Arabs who were keeping the oil from you, but since they owned the oil, it was easier to point an accusing finger at me. Your non-Jewish friends began to look askance at you and to say some not so nice things about me.

JUDAH: And I stuck up for you. Which is more than I can say for you and what you say about me.

ISRAEL: But that's precisely the difference I'm talking about. When I hear criticism of you, I don't feel attacked. I take it for what it is—that is, for criticism aimed at you. That's why I can judge it on its merits. As a minority, on the other hand, you take every critical remark about Jews anywhere as a personal affront. It doesn't matter if the Jews concerned live in Israel, Morocco, or France. That's why you were made so uncomfortable by what was said about me. No one actually told you that you were responsible for Israel's actions, but that's what the eyes of your non-Jewish friends seemed to say. After all, you didn't mind sharing the credit for those actions when they went down well with the world.

The ogre of anti-Semitism that you're so afraid of began to raise its ugly head. And it was all my fault. It was me who had gotten you into this mess. Little by little you began to speak in a voice you hadn't used before the Yom Kippur War. I was no longer the omnipotent hero. Irving Howe, a leading Jewish intellectual, wrote an article in January 1974 predicting the possible destruction of the state of Israel. This was a possibility no Jew had ever considered, let alone written about, before the Yom Kippur War. Why are the intellectuals silent in the face of this horrible possibility, Howe asked. Because "it's no longer fashionable to be so passionately involved in the fate of Israel." The author and editor, Marie Syrkin, reacted to this article by describing the response of Jewish intellectuals to the Yom Kippur War as "at most one of restrained concern or even indifference . . . the intellectual community refrained from openly and unequivocally taking a stand on the side of Israel, which was the victim of an attack, even though the fate of the Jewish state was at stake."* And what was the reason? Because of "the fatigue from the struggle for the sake of Israel." Philip Klutznik, the former president of B'nai B'rith, said immediately after the end of the war that American Jews "must be aware of the danger of being too preoccupied with Israel."† Not really a new opinion, but one that was given great impetus by the war.

JUDAH: And that's what brought about the change? Only the Yom Kippur War? Have you really forgotten other events or do you just prefer not to remember them? Do I need to remind you about the *Intifada?* Do I have to refresh your memory about the shooting of Palestinian children by Israeli soldiers, the beating of women, the torture of prisoners and other acts that have almost become normal? Have you forgotten the invasion of Lebanon, that turned into your Vietnam? The massacre in the Sabra and Shatilla refugee camps near Beirut to which you were a party in silence if not in deed? Or the affair of Jonathan Pollard, which showed you up as a schlemiel and ingrate and exposed me to the classical charge of dual loyalty?

---

* *Davar,* February 4, 1974.
† *Ha'aretz,* September 20, 1973.

ISRAEL: I accept the fact that all of these have contributed to the change in your attitude, but I continue to argue that the process began after the Yom Kippur War. Since that war, you never stop telling us what to do. For example, in a meeting between Zalman Shoval, the Israeli ambassador in Washington, and the heads of the Presidents Conference (September 22, 1991), all those present told the ambassador that Israel's settlement policy is a "catastrophe in Israel–U.S. relations and a catastrophe to the position of the Jewish community." We Israelis differ in our thoughts about the settlements, but does the "position" of American Jews also have to be considered? And if the settlements really are essential for Israel's security, should they then be discontinued to prevent impairing your "position." The chairman of the Presidents Conference took a moderate position: "U.S. Jewry understands Israel's policy on the settlements, but not the pace at which they are being established."* When the Israeli government hesitated about coming to the peace talks in Washington, Jewish leaders phoned Prime Minister Shamir and "urged him to recommend to the Cabinet that Israel come to the talks."† And after the government decided not to come (a decision that was later changed), one of the leaders said: "It's a nightmare. I never dreamt of such a thing in my worst dreams."

Later there was the affair of the guarantees Israel had requested for the sum of $10 billion to help absorb the Russian immigrants. As soon as Washington decided to link the guarantees to the settlements issue, the pressure

* *Ma'ariv,* February 24, 1991.
† *Ma'ariv,* September 24, 1991.

began. "I think that if within two weeks Israel doesn't arrive at an agreement about the guarantees, the chances of getting them will be very slim," said Malcolm Hoenline, executive director of the Presidents Conference of Jewish Organizations in the United States.*

Even public figures who identify themselves with the opposition to the Jewish establishment are not far behind, and sometimes way ahead, in voicing opinions and offering advice. One of the most prominent American Jews in this catagory is Michael Lerner, editor of the bimonthly Jewish publication *Tikkun*. What does Lerner have to contribute to the question of American aid and loan guarantees to Israel? In an editorial published in *Tikkun*'s July/August 1991 issue, he writes that he is "very reluctant to support any program of [U.S.] aid cuts." However, he continues, "economic pressure can take other forms," and he proposes such a strategy for Washington to use in taming the stubborn Israelis. He terms it "pressure through incentives." What does this mean in practical terms?

"My specific proposal is this: Let the U.S. publicly promise Israel that it will give 10 billion bollars of aid per year for five years. This aid . . . would be contingent upon Israel meeting two conditions: it must begin direct negotiations with Palestinian representatives . . . before the first year; and it must conclude an agreement for a demilitarized Palestinian state by the end of the second year of the aid."

Any unprejudiced reader can see that Lerner's well-meaning proposal places all the burden on Israel. How can Israel guarantee that these conditions will be met? Even if

* *Ma'ariv,* December 1, 1991.

we happen to agree that most of the time, Israel is in fact responsible for the many failures to reach an agreement with the Palestinians, it is equally clear to me that if I were a Palestinian I would want to do everything in my power to ensure that such agreements were *not* reached within the stipulated period. How can we account for this peculiar moral blindness on the part of an obviously intelligent man? Whenever I encounter such "sophisticated" thinking, I remember the Marquise de Merteuil's remark to the Vicomte de Valmont (in Christopher Hampton's play, *Les Liaisons Dangereuses*) expressing her opinion of a mutual acquaintance: "Like most intellectuals, he is intensely stupid."

And it's not only a question of political and security issues. No sooner had Rabbi Yitzhak Peretz, the minister of the interior, harshly criticized the nonobservance of Jewish tradition in the kibbutzim than the voice of an American rabbi, Daniel Sim, was heard—speaking on behalf of other leaders—saying that "Rabbi Peretz had got to go." Apparently, scores of Jewish leaders, big and small, know better than we do what is good for us. Indeed, when President Bush said in his famous speech that "little me has to stand alone to safeguard national American interests in the face of thousands of lobbyists," not only did I know what he meant, but I was able to identify with him.

JUDAH: I never said anything that you didn't say yourself even more outspokenly.

ISRAEL: You have children, don't you?

JUDAH: Two. That's the number we agreed on.

ISRAEL: Then you know that you sometimes lose your

temper at them and say some very harsh things that you would never let an outsider say, even in a much milder form.

JUDAH: I live in a country where the right to say what I think is basic. Are you suggesting that I waive it for you?

ISRAEL: I'm not questioning the right, I'm questioning your right to the right. I'm suggesting there should be no rights without obligations—and vice versa. Your country allows you to say what you think, but in return you're expected to obey the law, pay your taxes, serve in the army in wartime, etc.

In short, like all things, the right to say what you think has its price. And in my case, that's a price you don't want to pay. You want to acquire the right for less than nothing, and with all kinds of extras that I'll get around to later.

JUDAH: Perhaps you don't understand me. I never meant to suggest that my right to say what I think means you have to agree with me.

ISRAEL: I understand you perfectly, but what you said just now is a bit disingenuous. When you issue a public statement, or pass a resolution in one of your organizations, or publish an opinion piece in the newspaper to the effect that I should do such-and-such, do you really believe that's just saying what you think? You know very well that in practice voicing such opinions translates into pressure—into pressure from you and a clear signal to the administration in Washington that it too can lean on me without meeting resistance from the Jewish community. Don't get me wrong, please. I'm not talking about this or that specific policy of yours. I don't care whether it's dovish or hawkish. I object to you pressuring me in any direction at all.

JUDAH: But I always have your best interests at heart.

ISRAEL: I don't doubt it. It's just that you have your own interests even more at heart. Before you formulate a position, you ask yourself how it will sound to your non-Jewish neighbors. You're very anxious to get across the message that you aren't us: that you don't think like us, that you wouldn't behave like us, that they shouldn't resent you because of us.

JUDAH: Are you suggesting that I would knowingly harm you for my own benefit?

ISRAEL: Knowingly? What is knowingly? Suppose a politician does something that is against the national interest: grants a political appointment to an incompetent, for example, or, on a larger scale, urges his party to adopt unwise policies in order to gain power or remain in it. Is he knowingly harming his country? Not in the sense that he hasn't already convinced himself that the best thing for his country is that he and his party be in power. Any harm he causes, he is sure, is minor compared to that of surrendering power to a rival party or politician. The minute you can program yourself in this way, it's easy to do the most atrocious things in the name of the public welfare.

And that, on a different level, is exactly what has happened to you. If I can compare your brain to a computer, you first scan your program to see what is best for you and then find the reasons why that is best for us, too.

Take the question of the loan guarantees. Israel asked Washington for guarantees so it could obtain loans of $10

billion to help absorb immigration from the former Soviet
Union. The American administration decided to link its
decision to a demand that Israel stop building new
settlements on the West Bank. There are divergent opinions on this matter in Israel. But do American Jews really
know whether additional settlements are good or bad for
us? Do you even care? What you do know, and what really
interests you, is that if you support the Israeli position you
will get involved in a conflict with your government, and
you will be very unpopular with your recession-stricken
non-Jewish neighbors. So what do you do? Do you say that
you oppose the stand of Israel because it is damaging to you,
because it makes your life more difficult? In other words, do
you tell the truth? Of course not. Instead you say it's good
for me! Here's what Sally Gilbert, a Jewish leader from El
Paso, had to say to *The New York Times* (March 2, 1992):
"I basically feel that Bush and Baker are right. They are
holding up a mirror to Israel and saying take a look at
yourself. Those of us who want to see an Israel with a
healthier society and economy think this is the kick Israel
needs to get in order to build a better society." David W.
Belin, a Des Moines lawyer who runs a national organization
to counter Jewish intermarriage, also revealed his thoughts
to *The New York Times* (March 3, 1992), saying that "Israel
cannot remain a democracy holding territories occupied by
large amounts of Arabs." Apparently, you are not involved
at all. You have no motives of your own. It's me, and only
me, that you are worried about.

JUDAH: Don't you do the same thing?

ISRAEL: Of course I do. We all tend to rationalize what

is good for us. That's precisely why we should be wary of taking positions on other people's problems the price for whose solution we ourselves will not have to pay.

Let's take another example. When you tell me that I shouldn't employ violence against Arabs, what exactly do you mean? That you're humanly upset by it? Quite honestly, is it really the poor Arabs you feel sorry for? I don't remember you being so compassionate when I first conquered the territories, or even after that, until the Yom Kippur War made the occupation unpopular in the West.

JUDAH: It has nothing to do with the Yom Kippur War. It has to do with the *Intifada*. Before it broke out the world and I thought of you as an occupier too, but as an enlightened one.

ISRAEL: That's true. But what is it that bothers you about the fact that I'm no longer perceived as an enlightened occupier today? My beating Arabs or the beating taken by our own image? I'm thinking of the Jew from New Jersey who came to me after a talk I gave and said, "Look, killing a single Arab puts you on the front page of *The New York Times*, so if you have to kill one, why not kill a few hundred?" In other words, if you're damaging your image anyway, you may as well get the most out of it. Whose image was he talking about, mine or yours? I suppose mine—but would he care so much about mine if it didn't also reflect on his?

In a word, it's not our being crooks that bothers you, it's our getting caught. You don't mind our being barbarians as long as you don't have to hear the unflattering remarks of your non-Jewish friends about "those Israelis of yours."

To you that smells the same as "you Jews." You're upset with me because you think that the least I can do for you—the least I should do for you—is not to embarrass you in front of the Gentiles.

Michael Lerner says it very clearly in his *Tikkun* editorial (September/October 1991): "When I hear someone saying that Israelis are engaging in torture my back goes up and I want to say, 'It's not true.' But it is true, and the Jewish people both in Israel and around the world must acknowledge what is being done in our name." These are the key words, the words that matter to you more, much more, than any of my actions: *"in our name."*

That's why you're also upset with whoever brings my misdeeds to the attention of the public. And above all with the media, the root of all evil. The unfair, unbalanced, inaccurate, Jew-hostile media. Perhaps there's a grain of truth in all that, but that doesn't change the fact that when the news on TV shows a soldier hitting a child, that's exactly what happened: A soldier hit a child. To you it's a problem in public relations. Like a broken record you keep repeating that Israel has bad PR. Nothing can get it into your head that the best and most sophisticated PR in the world can't make a soldier hitting a child look like a defender of his country.

JUDAH: What are you smiling at?

ISRAEL: I just remembered a woman I met on a lecture tour in your Middle West. It was an evening in a home in a rich suburb to which fourteen guests were invited. I spoke about the *Intifada,* the political situation in Israel, the prospects for peace, etc. Twenty minutes and ten more for questions, followed by coffee and cake. That's when my hostess came over to me, a perfectly pleasant, intelligent, middle-aged woman. She wanted me to explain something about the *Intifada,* which I did, I thought, with scholarly exactitude, but when I was through she complained unhappily: "Yes, I understand the problem, but do we have to see Israeli soldiers shooting Arabs all the time on television?" "Would you rather it were the other way around?" I asked her. "Of course not," she answered—and I'm sure she meant it. You know what, though? It's a terrible thing to say, but I feel that unconsciously you would prefer that it were the other way around. Because then I would be the underdog, which would make you look better and win you a lot more sympathy. And if my being the underdog means my being on the receiving end of the stick, well, that's too bad, you wouldn't want me to be hit too hard or hurt too much, but it would be better than the way things are now.

JUDAH: What you are saying is not only terrible, but unfair and incorrect.

ISRAEL: Is that so? Let's go back to the Gulf War. What the Americans saw on their TV screens was not just planes bombing Baghdad or soldiers beating the enemy. They also saw Scud missiles falling on Israel, and cowed and frightened Israelis. And you, my dear brother, you reveled in an orgy of masochistic pleasure at my suffering since, despite the pain it caused you, it also raised my moral status and proved my political virtue as an ally of America. You only had one real concern during that time: that God forbid I should decide to retaliate, even though my

41

security depends largely upon my credibility in saying that
I *will* retaliate against any and all Arab attacks. For public
consumption, you said that I have the full right to do so;
but privately you told my leaders not to retaliate. Because
in that pose I was so photogenic and made you look so
good. That was just the kind of situation you dream about;
Israel taking a beating from the Arabs in a war in which
she's a passive American ally. That unprecedented situation enabled you to organize huge demonstrations on my
behalf, to send messages of encouragement, and to end-
lessly repeat your favorite punch line whenever I'm in
trouble: "The People of Israel Lives!"

It also enabled you to send the members of the Presidents Conference to visit me to demonstrate your solidarity. This is how their visit looked to a *Ma'ariv* journalist
(January 29, 1991):

"At 3:45 P.M., a policewoman sporting a punk haircut
shouted to a more clean-cut looking policeman: 'Stop the
traffic.' All the cars stopped, while members of the
Presidents Conference alighted from two buses and with
exemplary order lined up opposite the ruins of houses in
Ramat Gan that had been hit by Scud missiles. Immediately they pulled out their Japanese pocket cameras and
took each other's pictures against the background of the
ruins. . . . One of the evacuated residents, who had come
to rescue an enormous quantity of cans of corn from the
debris of his kitchen, gazed indifferently at the American
visitors. 'What, did they come here to plant a forest?' he
asked. 'It's the March of Dimes,' the policeman offered as
his own version of the visit. The leader of the delegation,
Mrs. Shoshana Cardin, graciously stated that she 'knows

she'll feel a moment of anxiety when she puts on a gas mask, but we must be here.' "

I doubt if Mrs. Cardin ever actually got the chance to experience the moment of anxiety she was so much looking forward to, because the presidents remained in Israel just forty-eight hours. After all, there is no need to exaggerate expressions of solidarity, especially in times of danger.

A survey conducted after the war by the American-Jewish Committee showed that on all controversial subjects, support for Israel's positions had grown; in particular there was a marked rise in identification with the state of Israel and the sense of loyalty to it: 31 percent compared to 22 percent the previous year. No, no, don't bother to answer. I know you will protest, you will deny, you will say that you suffered together with me, that you were worried about my fate during the war. Just drop it. Save those statements for the UJA speeches.

JUDAH: It's very hard to argue with emotions. But I'm not clear on your rational position. You fault me for leveling criticism. What about you? You sound as if the present state of affairs doesn't bother you one bit.

ISRAEL: It bothers me a great deal. And for some of the same reasons that it bothers you. I don't like to be seen by the world as a brutal conqueror. It's not my best feature, and no one likes to have his weak points displayed in public. I would like to have a better image, too. It would make my life easier in various ways—and besides, who doesn't want to be loved?

The difference between us, though, is that I have to worry about something far more serious: not the image of the occupation but the reality of its effect on us Israelis and our children as human beings. After all, images come and go and rarely have much to do with the facts. They're more a product of circumstances than of what one does or doesn't do. Do you really think we were so wonderful and enlightened in 1967? Nonsense. But the Arabs hadn't discovered their oil and petrodollar power yet, and we had still not lost a war. And so then we were the good guys and now we're the bad ones. Maybe in a few years' time we'll be the good guys again.

What the occupation is doing to us as human beings, however—that's something that threatens to wreak irreparable damage to the fabric of our lives while turning us into a brutal and insensitive society. Such a society is not one I would want to belong to. And yet you don't seem to be particularly bothered by that. Take the scandal a few years ago in Israel's General Security Service. It was a traumatic episode in which the Israeli media revealed that the director of the GSS had ordered two Palestinian terrorists killed without trial and had then lied to an official committee of inquiry. In several of my talks in the United States I expressed the opinion that, even if the episode damaged Israel's image abroad, it was crucial to bring it to light, because in a democratic society not even the security apparatus should be allowed to be above the law. Not a single American Jewish audience enjoyed hearing that. The almost universal reaction to what I said was: Yes, but why wash our dirty linen in public?

If that had happened in America, you would never have agreed to sweep such a thing under the rug. You would have demanded an investigation, a trial, the immediate dismissal of the guilty parties. When it comes to me, though, you expect—you practically demand—that I should say to hell with democratic principles. It's not so terrible if Israeli officials and government agencies take the law into their own hands. It's not good, but there are worse things. And one of these is a tarnished image.

Indeed, I sometimes think that as long as Israel's image in America remained decent and humane, you wouldn't care if in actual fact we were a society of cannibals!

JUDAH: That's a ridiculous thing to say. I wouldn't want to have anything to do with such a society.

ISRAEL: You wouldn't? Let's take two scenarios. The first is the present one. Within its 1967 borders Israel is a more or less civil society, free and democratic, whereas in the West Bank and Gaza Strip it is an occupying power performing acts of brutality that are certainly not a social norm but whose coverage in the press creates the impression that no Israeli goes to bed at night without maiming at least one Palestinian during the day.

Now let us imagine Israel as a hypothetical dictatorship in which news items about atrocities committed against Arabs and antigovernment Jews do not appear. Apart from some noteworthy medical advance or scientific discovery that we make, we simply don't make it into the American media. In other words, bad as we are, we look good. Which of these two scenarios would you prefer?

JUDAH: Why should I have to choose between them? Can't you think of a situation in which you would not only look good but be good? Is that beyond your powers of imagination?

ISRAEL: Yes, I think it is. And later I'll tell you why, because it has to do with our vicious circle. But you still haven't answered my question.

JUDAH: I think most of us would prefer "the open society" to the other alternative. But I don't think that's relevant. Your question proves that you haven't the foggiest notion of what it's like to come to the office the morning after a TV news clip of your soldiers beating women and children. You don't understand what it's like to be looked at out of the corners of all those eyes and to put up with all those snide comments. There's no point in trying to explain it to you. You have to take my word for it that it is very, very difficult. You have to understand that what you do does affect me. I don't think it's too much to expect that you take this into account when making your decisions.

ISRAEL: I think you should relieve me of the obligation to make your life more comfortable and let me decide what is right in terms of my own existence and survival. If you can't lend a hand, at least stay out of my way.

Don't tell me what law to pass about who is a Jew. Don't tell me you don't want to invest in me because I am an insufferable bureaucrat and that you expect me to change my ways. Don't tell me how to treat security detainees. Don't ask me to take one or another political position to please your government. Don't expect me to build my life according to the model you want in order to help and please you. And please don't tell me who my friends and my enemies are. That is something I can decide for myself.

But it's clear to me that the expectation gap between us

can't be bridged, which brings me to the third and last reason for being against your right to criticize me or give me advice. It's the most important reason of all: the fact that it's a right without obligations and that you're not asked to pay any price for it.

JUDAH: I never pressure you to accept policies that may be inimical to your welfare.

ISRAEL: How do you know? What makes you so sure that you know what's inimical and what isn't? Suppose, for example, that under pressure from you I withdraw from all the Occupied Territories and a year later a war breaks out which I lose or am badly beaten in—what then? Or suppose you pressure me into not withdrawing, and consequently the same thing happens?

JUDAH: What then? We'd help you!

ISRAEL: You don't say. What would you do about it?

JUDAH: I would use all my influence to make the United States intervene.

ISRAEL: How?

JUDAH: Militarily, if necessary.

ISRAEL: Oh, yes: the way it intervened before the Six Day War? I was threatened with destruction then, too, don't forget. I even had a guarantee that if my coasts were blockaded, the United States would run the blockade. Of course, it didn't. Such guarantees have a way of disappearing at critical moments. As our prime minister at the time, Levi Eshkol, used to say to anyone complaining to him that he hadn't kept a promise: "It's true that I promised, but I never promised to keep my promise."

JUDAH: I can't imagine that the United States, that the world . . ."

ISRAEL: I believe I've heard those words before. Can you guarantee that the United States, especially after the lesson of Vietnam, will send its youth to fight for me? And what moral right do I have to demand such a thing from a nice American youngster? How about you yourself—would you come to fight by my side? Would you send your children to do it?

JUDAH: I know that I would do everything I could to help.

ISRAEL: Let's see what your everything means. You would holler, give speeches, issue proclamations, exert pressure. You would also be grief-stricken. I have no doubt of it. You would lament my sad fate, give me the most moving eulogies—but not one hair of your head would be endangered. Despite your grief, you wouldn't call off your Caribbean vacation. And your children would go back to college in the fall while mine lay dead or wounded in a war that might not have broken out, or might have ended differently, if not for your pressure on me.

And above all you would express your regret and your commitment to continued participation in the way you know best, the way you are used to, employing the tool you built for the purpose: the money machine.

2

The Money Machine

Buy Yourself a Jew

JUDAH: What tool are you talking about? What is this "money machine" you refer to?

ISRAEL: I am talking about the vast, sophisticated monster that sends its numerous long arms into the pockets of its victims on the basis of hypocritical and mendacious claims. I am talking about the United Jewish Appeal, the Israel Bonds, the Jewish National Fund, the Friends of the Hebrew University of Jerusalem, the Friends of the Tel Aviv University, the Friends of Haifa Technion, the Friends of Ben-Gurion University, not to mention the National Museum in Jerusalem, and countless yeshivas and synagogues. I am talking about a machine whose driving force is the urge for *schnor,** which is equally strong among the giver and the receiver.

JUDAH: You mean the American Jewish fund-raising bureaucracy? Why are you so resentful about that? After all, its aim is to help. Why do you think I establish and keep all these organizations going? Why do you think I waste my valuable time on all this activity?

ISRAEL: No doubt you have more than one reason. For one thing, you think it legitimates your claim to be my partner. It also makes you feel powerful and superior. My generals may be smart and brave, but in the end they come begging to you, which gives you the kick of being ultimately more of a success than they are.

But the main reason you send money, it seems to me, is that you still don't feel safe in the country that you live in.

---

* An expectation of charity based on a pretense of merit, to the point where it becomes a way of life.

51

No matter how much a part of American society you feel, you can't rule out the possibility of unexpected developments. One doesn't have to think of Nazi Germany to imagine situations in which your life could be made difficult, even intolerable. And if that should ever happen, it's good to know there's a safe house you can always escape to. You're relieved to have an option that the Jews of Europe didn't. I'm your insurance company, and you make your payments to me just as you do on your car insurance, your home insurance, your life insurance. But as your insurance company I don't even have the privilege of setting my own premiums and conditions. It's you, the insured, who do that—and every year you lower them more.

JUDAH: You've got your facts wrong. There has hardly been a year in which I didn't raise more money than the year before. In 1990 I raised for the United Jewish Appeal approximately $720 million in regular campaign funds and last year this figure grew to $750 million.

ISRAEL: I'm not talking about how much you raise. I'm talking about how much I get, which is less than half, and the gap between the two keeps growing.

JUDAH: That certainly isn't true of Israel bonds. You keep every penny that I pay for them.

ISRAEL: Every penny that you pay, eh? You're right. I do get every penny of it—which is to say, every penny of practically nothing. Let's take a look at how they work, these Israel government bonds, because they're the biggest scam in Jewish philanthropy.

Here's what happens. Let's say you buy a million dollars

worth of bonds. You then go and sell them, taking as a tax loss the difference between their dividend on the free market and the dividend of ordinary bonds. With that money you go and buy more bonds. That way you can get up at gala evenings and announce huge purchases of Israel bonds when your only real expense is the difference between the interest borne by them and the interest borne by other bonds, part of which is paid for by the United States Internal Revenue Service.

So much for what you give.

And what do I get?

First of all, I have to pay you 4.5 percent interest on individually purchased bonds and a bit more on large purchases made by big organizations like pension funds. So far, so good, because if I wanted a loan on the free market, the interest I would be charged would be slightly higher. At first glance, that makes it worth my while.

But only at first glance. Because the fact is that those bonds cost me overhead. And it's not chicken feed, either: We're talking about thirty million dollars a year! When you add that to the interest I pay, it turns out that the bonds are costing me as much if not more than a loan on the free market.

JUDAH: Then why go on selling them?

ISRAEL: For the sake of the overhead! Shall I tell you what that goes for? Titles and positions of power such as chairperson, president, vice president, and so on; travel and entertainment expenses for Israeli cabinet ministers, Knesset members, generals, executives, journalists—hundreds and hundreds of them who go on American lecture tours every year with their plane tickets, their first-class hotels, their fancy restaurants, and all their other expenses paid; and a huge bureaucracy of office workers and executives with fat salaries and handsome expense accounts.

Look at the bonds operation and you'll see a classic example of an institution that ceased long ago to serve the goal it was established for and now exists only for its own sake. And also to allow certain very rich Jews who don't like giving away money to keep up appearances by telling you, "But why are you hounding me for a contribution? I've already bought bonds!"

In a nutshell, the bonds cost you next to nothing and are worth next to nothing to me. At least we come out even.

That's more than I can say for the United Jewish Appeal. In this case you really do give more, but I get less and less all the time.

In the old days I really received all the money you gave me, because it was given via organizations that existed exclusively for that purpose. One fine day, though, you went and combined those organizations with other organizations that raised funds for your local needs. That in itself was inexcusable, because it meant that under the pretext of raising money for Israel you were collecting funds meant for other purposes, too.

And not only did you hoodwink your own contributors, you hoodwinked me also. At first the cut you agreed to give me was more or less the same as the percentage raised for me before the organizations were merged. That worked out to about 80 percent for me and about 20 percent for you. Subsequently, though, you raised your share steadily and lowered mine. You go on collecting the money in my name, but I see less of it from year to year. And you haven't even bothered to consult me about it. You've appointed yourself the sole judge of how much you skim off from what's given to me.

JUDAH: To me, to you—you make it sound as though the money that stays in America works against you. But that money goes to communal projects such as old age homes, aid to the needy, and above all, Jewish education—that is, to raising our children's Jewish consciousness and ensuring that they grow up as Jews. That's important for the Jewish people and it's important for you, because the more Jewish they feel, the more connected to you they'll feel, too.

ISRAEL: Let's leave Jewish education and its benefits for later. But if that's what the money is for, why not come out and say it? Why collect it in my name and at my expense? Don't all these things matter enough for you to want to fund them anyway?

JUDAH: Of course they do, and I mention them in all my campaigns.

ISRAEL: In inverse proportion to how the money is divided. Your UJA rallies spend two or three minutes discussing local needs and half-an-hour or more discussing Israel's, because you know that nothing is more soporific than talking about Jewish education and old age homes. Israel, with all its big generals and politicians, is much sexier. And so you sell your clients a bill of goods and tell them that the money is for me.

The trouble is, though, that even the sexiest woman loses her charms over the years, so that you have to keep adding all kinds of come-ons if you still want to sell her. And when it comes to come-ons, you're hard to beat.

Every year you look for a new gimmick to build your campaign on. It starts with the crucial decision to run a "one-line campaign" or a "two-line campaign." A one-liner is an ordinary campaign. A two-liner is reserved for an emergency appeal. In a two-liner the pledge cards that you hand out to your victims have two lines at the bottom, one for the regular campaign and one for the special one.

The whole trick, of course, is to find a strong second bottom line that will pry open pockets. The best one—it's so good that it all but rips the pockets right out of your pants—is a war. Unfortunately, you can't count on a war every year. You have to go with your second best, which is Jews In Trouble.

Take Ethiopian Jews, for example. The year they were brought to Israel in Project Moses was an excellent one for you. It wasn't quite as good as a war year, but it came close. After all, it was so dramatic, so romantic. Planes taking off under cover of darkness from Addis Ababa, carrying people who had hardly ever seen a car. Planes coming and going continuously for several days and nights, until the last of these people was put on board. This drama had all the right elements—the fulfillment of Jewish destiny, the rescue of Jews in distress, the realization of a humanitarian cause, bringing people from the darkness of the Middle Ages into the light of civilization. And what a beautiful slogan you gave the campaign: You could buy yourself a Jew! Irresistible! How much did such a Jew cost? Six thousand dollars by your reckoning. "You don't know how lucky you are," the message went out at all your gatherings, "to be able to save Jewish lives. Just imagine if during the Hitler years . . .", etc., etc.

It was an offer you couldn't refuse. In America, where you can buy almost anything—a house, a car, a color TV, a video, a summer home—you now had a chance to add a Jew to your shopping list. Or several Jews, like the contributor who, after checking the price, reportedly told his local UJA chairman, "Okay, put me down for four *shvartzes.*"

JUDAH: But it worked. You may not like how we did it, but you received a lot of money to help you absorb those immigrants.

ISRAEL: Forty thousand five hundred Ethiopian Jews immigrated since 1977. And for this whole romantic drama that so stirred you, you sent about $60 million, a very small percentage of the overall sum this immigration and its problematic absorption cost and is still costing. Certainly not as much as your victims intended us to get. Because you pull a fast one with your emergency appeals as well. What happens? Often the contributor writes his entire pledge on the second line, because he wants all of it to go for that purpose. Innocent lamb that he is, he thinks that if there's a space to write down his preference, that preference will be honored. He doesn't know—and no one bothers to tell him—that you allocate his money as you please. Even if somebody gives his whole pledge to the Jews of Ethiopia, like, for example, the man who bought four of them, you take 60 percent for yourself and pass on only 40 percent to them. And that swindle is carried out in my name!

But that isn't the worst of it. After all, all you did was take money meant for me and keep it for yourself. That's nothing

compared to what you did for many years with the Jews of
the Soviet Union. There you outdid yourself, because you
took money meant for me and used it against me.

JUDAH: What are you talking about? We used the money
to help Russian refugees.

ISRAEL: To help them to do what? To go to America!
Granted, you've changed your policy now, but all through
the eighties I told you that I needed those Jews, I
practically begged you for them. And what did you do?
You took money collected in my name, money that was
supposed to help Israel, and spent it on bringing Soviet
Jews to America and robbing me of what I needed most!

JUDAH: That's not so. I staged a special campaign with the
slogan "Passage to Freedom."

ISRAEL: Everything you managed to raise in that campaign
amounted to less than $20 million. You were very disap-
pointed. You needed a lot more money. So how did you
make up the missing sum? From the current donations to
the UJA.

And that isn't all. There's still other money meant for
me that you keep 100 percent of. You don't let me have a
penny of it.

JUDAH: What are you talking about?

ISRAEL: About endowment funds willed to the UJA. There
are three billion dollars in those funds. The dividends from
them—hundreds of millions of dollars a year—stay entirely
with you. I don't get a red cent, though the money was
willed to an organization of which I am supposed to be a
senior partner.

So you tell me: What do I need all this for?

JUDAH: Because when all is said and done, you wind up with a very nice pile.

ISRAEL: I do? Shall I tell you how much that is? When the state of Israel was established, the money I got from you was 50 percent of my gross national product. Do you know what it is today? 0.02 percent! In 1989–90 I received $244 million out of the $750 million you collected in my name—that is, thirty-four cents on each dollar! What kind of money is that? By juggling two paragraphs in my national budget I can come up with such a sum in a fingersnap! Israel's foreign currency reserves alone add up to a billion dollars today, so what's 244 million?

To tell you the truth, I actually lose on it. Your Jewish Agency operates under an Israeli government charter that exempts it from all taxes except for VAT. If the agency paid taxes like any other organization in Israel, the Israeli government would take in annually more money than you send me—and for that you expect me to say thank you!

JUDAH: But even if the money is insignificant to you, you can't deny that it's a personal sacrifice to give it.

JUDAH: I can't? All right, let's have a look. Financial sacrifice, after all, is a relative thing. It's not the absolute sum of the contribution that counts but the percentage of the contributor's income. If a man with an income of two hundred dollars pledges one hundred, he's sacrificing more than a man with an income of a thousand who pledges two hundred, am I right?

JUDAH: That's obvious.

ISRAEL: Good. Tell me, then, what percent of your income

do you give to Israel every year? Half a percent? One percent? Maybe 2 percent? I give at least 55 percent.

JUDAH: You're talking about your taxes. I'm talking about a contribution I make after paying taxes.

ISRAEL: Have it your way. Add it up. Take your taxes and your contribution together: What percentage of your income do they come to? 25 percent? 30 percent? 35 percent? And we're talking about an income that is at least twice as large as mine.

JUDAH: I give as much as I can.

ISRAEL: Don't be so modest. There are today in America over 300,000 Jewish households with an annual income of more than $1 million. Only a third of them—one out of three!—gives over a thousand dollars annually to the UJA. The rest contribute less or nothing at all. And yet at the same time, huge and steadily growing amounts of Jewish money are donated annually for non-Jewish purposes. In 1981 Walter Annenberg alone donated $150 million to the Corporation for Public Broadcasting. This past year he gave $15 million for the absorption of Soviet refugees in Israel and $50 million to some purely American institution. When Jack Linsky died in 1982, do you know whom he willed $50 million to? The UJA? A new hospital in Israel? No, sir. He gave that little boodle to the Metropolitan Museum of Art. In 1986 Milton Petrie donated $10 million for cancer research.

JUDAH: I don't get it. First you tell me you don't want my money and now you're upset that I keep it in America.

ISRAEL: I have nothing against your keeping it in America. What I'm against is the hoo-ha you make over all the money you give me. Just to keep things in their right proportion, bear in mind that no American Jew ever gave $50 million to Israel or to any Jewish cause. Not even when Israel was fighting for its life.

JUDAH: Giving to non-Jewish causes enables us to give to Israel. You wouldn't want the Gentiles to think we're ingrates who owe America everything yet only take care of our own.

ISRAEL: Look at the Mormons. There are less of them than of you—only 4 million. Do you know how much they raise every year? Two billion dollars! Not a penny of it goes to non-Mormon causes. Have you heard any complaints about them lately?

JUDAH: Anti-Semitism has greater roots in America than anti-Mormonism. The Mormons are still Christians, after all.

ISRAEL: Look, I honestly think that charity begins at home. It's you who keeps telling me how much I matter to you. But as you protest your love, I think you should remember how relative your sacrifice is to mine. This big money machine of yours, it doesn't exist for me. It's you who need it and you who want it. It permits you to hold conferences, to travel to Israel, and to engage in various social activities at which you can talk about poor little Israel and your needy brothers there who mustn't be forgotten.

I have no end of admiration for the patience you have for preaching and listening. You've been saying and hearing the same things for decades and you know that most of them are no longer relevant, but each time you pretend all over again that they're exciting news. Or am I wrong? Perhaps many of you are no longer so willing to pretend. Perhaps the time has come for you to reconsider if this is really the best way to maintain your Jewishness. If you did, you might discover that for every Jew you hold onto in this way, you lose many more by being interested only in their pockets.

PLAYING THE LEADERSHIP GAME

ISRAEL: I'm afraid, though, that I'm being naive. You won't reconsider, because your leaders won't allow you to. That's a reckoning they won't let you make, because it's the money machine that has made them leaders. It's in their own personal interest that the name of the leadership game should continue to be money. Not intelligence, not intellectual achievement, not talent, and certainly not Jewish or Zionist commitment. Just money. Do you want to be a leader? Give more than anyone else. Jewish leadership in America isn't earned and it certainly isn't elected; it's bought. And not at such a high price. For far less than the price of an original Chagall, any fabrics dealer or whisky distiller in America can buy himself practically free admission to the White House. For slightly more than the price of one of his vacation homes, any manufacturer who produces enough underpants can purchase the attentions of senators and governors. For the price of the furniture in one of those homes, you can buy yourself a meeting with the prime minister of Israel and/or any of his ministers whenever you decide you have the time for them.

I think it's an excellent investment. In fact, I think it's the best investment there is today in the world of politics and business. To become a political figure in the United States you have to undertake arduous and onerous election campaigns and even then you're never sure you'll be elected. Jewish leaders have no such problems. They've made life easy for themselves. Give money, get leadership.

I'm reminded of the Jewish billionaire who was upset by our Israeli electoral system because he didn't like the extraordinary power it gave to small, marginal parties. And so he proposed donating a few million to the University of Tel Aviv to set up a research institute to investigate other electoral systems and recommend the one best suited for Israel. Everything went smoothly until someone gently asked him at a meeting whether, before changing the electoral system in Israel, he didn't think there should be a system for electing Jewish leaders in America. The billionaire stalked out with an angry look and that was the last of his donation.

Had he seen it through, it would have been a wonderful example of wasted money, because research has nothing to do with changing the electoral system in Israel. Were finding a better system the problem, the system we have now would have been changed long ago, just as elections would have been held in the American Jewish community if it were a question of knowing how to hold them. Neither of these things has happened because the people who could make them happen haven't wanted them to. Only the Knesset can change Israel's electoral system, but that's the system that elected the members of the Knesset in the first place, so what can be so bad about it? If anything can bring about a change, it is massive public pressure in Israel itself, and not donations for research.

The same goes for you. Changing the system that brought your present leadership to power means sawing off the branch on which it's sitting, so why do it? After all, over the years several attempts were made to enable the Jews to elect their representatives, but they all failed. Why? Because it's not possible? Because the Jews don't know how to do it? Certainly not. The reason is that it's a lot simpler to give a few million as a donation, one you would give anyway and that is recognized as an expense for tax purposes, than to spend additional sums of money on an election campaign which may not succeed. The result is that practically all of your leaders are wealthy businessmen or professionals. The president of the World Jewish Congress is Edgar Bronfman, an American whiskey baron. The president of the Zionist Organization of America, W. James Schiller, is a certified public accountant and business consultant. Kent Shiner, president of B'nai B'rith, is an insurance executive and financial consultant. The president of the American Jewish Congress, Robert Lifton, is cochairman of the Marcade Group, and Marvin Lender, whose title is "professional businessman," is national chairman of the United Jewish Appeal. These are all shrewd people who know all too well that it is easier to tell Israelis to elect their leaders differently than to have to stand for election in America itself.

It's not me who needs the money machine, then—it's you and your leaders. There's no difference between leaders of organizations that define themselves as Zionist and leaders of non-Zionist organizations. And it's you who have made it into the ugly and corrupting monster that it is. You no longer even control it. It controls you and makes both you and me do things we ought to feel ashamed of.

JUDAH: Excuse me, but I fail to see what business it is of yours. You can say you don't like how the money is divided, you can even say you don't want it—but how I collect it is my own affair and doesn't concern anyone else.

ISRAEL: You couldn't be more wrong. My problem—our problem—isn't how much money I get or how fairly it's divided. The problem is the machine you've created for collecting this money. The problem is what this machine does to both of us. That's why it's my affair, too.

You've created a ruthless, well-oiled machine whose only aim is to collect money and that will do anything to do so. Every year you give its operators a higher quota to meet and tell them to stop at nothing to meet it. It's not a machine for weaklings. If you can't meet your quota, you're out. The only gauge of success, the one bottom line, is how many dollars you've brought in.

JUDAH: Perhaps you've gone far enough.

ISRAEL: If we stop here, it was pointless to begin. The only reason for having this conversation is to bare our chests. To sweep out from under the rug all that's collected there over the years.

JUDAH: What for? To give ammunition to our enemies?

ISRAEL: I think we give them ammunition when we do these things in the first place, not when we talk about them.

The mentality of the bottom line has engendered various forms of pressure, some simple and some highly sophisticated. Before getting to them, though, it should be pointed out that we are talking strictly about small-time Jews, that is, about Jews who are moderately wealthy or less. The big-timers, that is, the very rich Jews, are untouchable. You don't dare fool around with them. You use them to bait the line for the less rich Jews. You use their houses, their names, the desire of the less wealthy to associate with them. Even if they don't give themselves, or give much less than you know they can afford, you treat them with deference.

Many extremely rich Jews have learned their lesson and know that if you're wealthy enough, prestige and status come practically free. These are the people who get up at the gala dinners and announce enormous pledges. Afterwards they give what they want, often much less than they pledged. Some don't give at all. They know that no one will blow the whistle on them. They're not the object of the money machine. It's the Jews with less who are.

The first thing to be decided in approaching such a Jew is how much he can be asked for. In order to arrive at such an estimate, you need information about his income and his assets. To get such information you take liberties that would be considered a gross infringement of civil rights if taken by the IRS. The intelligence network that you've created for gathering it would be a credit to any secret service. It includes friends, neighbors, relatives, business associates. They tell you what you need to know about the victim: how many houses he owns, how many rooms there are in each house, when he last refurbished them, how much money it cost him, what his business brings in, what his net earnings last year were—everything. It's all stored in a computer that is updated with each new campaign.

On the basis of this data you decide how much your victim will be asked to "contribute." In a polite, friendly manner he is informed of the sum. If he agrees at once, there is no problem. This, however, happens rarely. Not many Jews will part with their money before they give you a good run for it. "Why don't you try my neighbor first, he's richer than I am." "I'd rather wait to see what my partner gives." "I'll think about it and give you an answer next week." Their attitude toward you is ambivalent. On the one hand, they complain that you're hounding them. On the other hand, they like the attention and know that once they've given they won't see or hear from you until the next campaign. They want to squeeze out of the situation every drop of attention and flattery that they can. If, having gotten it, they finally agree to your assessment— well and good. If not, the bargaining begins. If it ends successfully—good enough. But what happens if the victim still refuses to knuckle under and tells you to get lost? That's when you embark on a course of action designed to convince him to never again be so foolish.

It begins in the social domain. The news that the victim has refused to cooperate gets around. Not to everyone. Just to the right ears. That is, to the rich ones. In the society you've spawned, they're the only ones that matter.

Suddenly the victim finds himself invited to fewer social affairs, both private and public. Once his local UJA chairperson think he's gotten the hint, he's visited again. If he's amenable—all is forgiven. But suppose he continues to hold out?

The pressure now shifts to the business sector. Suddenly the victim finds that there's less demand for his products or services. And not just from Jewish buyers, either. The wealthy operators of the money machine have connections with non-Jews who depend on them, too, and can be counted on to cooperate. Nothing is ever said in so many words, but it isn't difficult to get the message across to a seasoned businessman, Jewish or Gentile, that Tycoon X, the head of the local campaign, would appreciate his transferring his business to someone else.

The next visit from his campaign leader finds the victim less unyielding. He may be a miser or a man of principle, but he isn't a fool. It's better to give in than to risk losing his social and commercial position.

Other kinds of pressure are simpler and more direct. Like making it clear, for instance, that admission to the local country club involves a campaign contribution as large as one's membership dues. Far away in Israel I'll receive a few more dollars because you love playing golf.

But such pressure is only one means, and a simple and vulgar one at that. You're sophisticated enough to know that it's neither possible nor necessary to use it all the time. Human beings, thank goodness, have other weaknesses that can be exploited. Such as the fact that it's human nature, Jewish nature, too, to like to give. But though giving is touted as the greatest of satisfactions, receiving is an even greater one. So if you can combine the small pleasure of giving with the far bigger one of getting, what could possibly be better?

The best way to achieve this is by grouping your victims by professional categories. You select young businessmen in their thirties and forties, men just starting out or in the process of getting ahead. These are your most problematic

types, because they tend to be so involved with their
careers that they have no time to see the light. Next you
divide them into professions. Let's say that one of these is
clothing manufacturing. You put together a group of
clothing manufacturers and suggest bringing them to
Israel for a ten-day tour. After all, you tell them, it's time
they saw their ancient homeland for themselves. Of course,
not all of them are convinced that that's how they want to
spend their vacation time. They haven't been to Italy yet,
they haven't even been to Hawaii—and besides, how can
they afford to go anywhere? How can they take time off
from a race in which there is no hope for the slackers and
the loafers?

"But look here," you say to them, "this is part of the
race. In fact, it's not only part of it, it's a good way of
getting ahead in it."

"Oh, yeah?" they say. "How's that?"

"What do you mean, how's that?" you reply with a
secretive smile. "For ten whole days you'll be only with
your associates. Just try to find another place where you'll
make so many intensive contacts so fast."

That's a language they understand. They'll come back
from their tour of the homeland with a new network of
relationships cemented by shared experience, two thousand years of Jewish heritage, and patriotic emotions they
never knew they had. A hundred dinners and lunches
could never have given them so many and such close ties.
What's ten or twenty thousand dollars a year compared to
the profits these make possible? You won't find many
better investments. (Especially since this one is partly tax
deductible!)

So far we've been talking about lateral ties, with fellow businessmen in the same league as yourself. But let's not forget the vertical ties, too. Way up on top of the money machine are the really wealthy Jews, men like Max Fisher and Edgar Bronfman. Suppose you come to a young lawyer on the make and say to him, "Hey, if you get on board you're not only joining the club of the Jewish people, you're joining an exclusive group of businessmen, too. You get to be a colleague of Bronfman's." (Wink.) Ordinarily speaking, he has as much chance of meeting Bronfman as of winning the Florida lottery. But if he joins, he's in. He'll meet Bronfman on social occasions; he'll meet him at conferences; he can dial his number any time he wants and say, "Hi, Edgar, can you spare me five minutes?"

You explain, you wink, you threaten, you cajole—but how exactly do you do it? What is the right time and place for it? Not to worry. Dozens of years of experience have established clear guidelines of Do's and Don't's. Tell me if they sound familiar.

Don't's

- Never visit your victim in his office, because that's the one place where he's God and you're just another beggar.
- If you run into your victim at the synagogue, you can mention Israel's problems and financial needs in a general sort of way but it's in poor taste to put the touch on him there.
- The telephone is an anti-Semitic instrument. Never use it for fund-raising, because if you do, you don't look serious.

Do's

- Telephones are allowable for scheduling a meeting. If you ask for "an hour or an hour-and-a-half" of your victim's time, you

give him the message that it's important and that he is too.
- The time of day you meet him is crucial. Breakfasts are iffy, because you never know if he slept well at night or what kind of mood he got up in. They're better than dinners, though, because after a hard day's work your victim can easily think of half-a-dozen things he'd like to do more than sit and talk about how much money he's going to hand over to you.

    The ideal time to meet is for lunch.
- The best place to meet is a small restaurant. Make sure there's no background music and that the tables are far apart. Stay away from anyplace where you'll have to shout to make yourself heard.
- Make it eyeball to eyeball. It's a must to let your victim see your sorrowful eyes when he tells you how much he's ready to pledge.

JUDAH: Everything you've said simply adds up to the fact that I'm an excellent fund-raiser. If you understood the way Americans think, you wouldn't be so sarcastic. For better or for worse, that's how it's done in the United States—and not just among Jews, either.

ISRAEL: Perhaps, but Jews have certainly made it into a fine art, and with unparalleled results. Especially since you don't stick to conventional methods or to the narrow borders of America. You have no limits at all, geographic, Jewish, or moral. When it comes to worming your way into your victims' pockets, nothing is sacred.

JUDAH: What on earth are you talking about?

ISRAEL: I'm talking about Auschwitz.

Along with most of the human race, you watched in amazement as the Iron Curtain lifted. You were gladdened —you were moved—perhaps you even shed a tear like many of us. But being merely a neutral observer is not for you.

71

Even when they're full of tears, your eyes never stop probing like radar for the possible benefits in a new situation. It didn't take you long to detect the potential of Auschwitz. In no time you had a new itinerary. Instead of New York–Tel Aviv, it was New York–Auschwitz–Tel Aviv.

JUDAH: Would you please tell me what is wrong with encouraging Jews to visit Auschwitz?

ISRAEL: I'm all for Jews seeing Auschwitz. I think that Auschwitz is the most concrete explanation there is of what Jewishness and Zionism are about. But that's not the only reason, or even the main one, that you bring your Jews there. "Do you see those tens of thousands of shoes that belonged to those who died here? Do you realize that hundreds of thousands of children were murdered here? Do you see the gas chambers? All this was done by the Nazis."

There's nothing wrong with that either. It's Jewish education at its best. It's just that you don't stop there. You go on: "Can any of you be sure, absolutely sure, that it won't happen again, even in the United States? What you see here is the reason the state of Israel is so important to us." To which, too, I have no objection. It's just that this whole, almost passionately Zionist speech merely serves as a build-up for the punch line: "Do you understand now why your pledge is so crucial? Do you understand why it has to be bigger this year?"

If the victim is a new one, you use the same means for slightly different ends. Having come to an agreement with him how great the Nazi horror was, you steer the conversation to your victim's annual income, his business profits, his property. The poor devil doesn't dare refuse to answer.

72

In fact, he's so shocked and frightened that he's dying to cooperate. And you, old pro that you are, write it all down in a little notebook and—once you've figured out what your victim's pledge should be, of course—dictate it to your secretary back in the office for entry in his personal file.

There's not another organization in the world that is as professional as you at milking money from catastrophe. When Palestinian terrorists murdered Israeli children in the town of Ma'alot, you came out in the *Baltimore Jewish Times* with a huge UJA ad that said: "Ma'alot-Auschwitz." Apart from the vulgarity of exploiting such a tragedy for fund-raising, the equation is historically and factually misleading. In Auschwitz, after all, Jews were led like sheep to the slaughter, while in Israel they can defend themselves. What would you have said had *The New York Times* published an editorial comparing the two? You would have attacked it bitterly for anti-Semitically seeking to minimalize what happened at Auschwitz. And you would have been right!

Yes, you know the difference as well as anyone, but what won't you do to shake out your victims' pockets? For so lofty a goal you're perfectly willing to portray my country as a place in which only a madman would want to live. Because what sane person would agree to live in Auschwitz?

THE TRAINED BEAR

ISRAEL: You embarrass me with your professional cynicism, your jadedness, your lack of inhibition. You embarrass me as a Jew. You embarrass me as an Israeli.

And you embarrass me as a human being.

Because it's not just my country and its values that have been yoked by you to your money machine. It's my countrymen, too.

You've made us your clowns, your vaudeville act.

You've even done it to our official representatives. To our diplomatic corps, for example. Generally, a consul's job is to issue visas, conduct public relations, and develop economic and cultural ties with local authorities— generally, that is, unless he happens to represent the Jewish state, in which case he functions also, and perhaps primarily, as a representative to the local Jewish community. Even if that were not the original intention—and it is—the reality leaves him no choice.

Indeed, an Israeli consul is not even a representative. In effect he is the local Jewish community's employee and entertainer. Every organization feels free to invite him to every function, no matter how large or small, so that the invitation can state that the Israeli consul is sponsoring it. The provender at such gatherings is invariable: 500 rolls, 250 salads, 50 chickens, 250 desserts—and one Israeli consul. Or ambassador. Or minister. Or—if it's a particularly gala occasion—Abba Eban.

And the representatives of Israel go along with it. Consuls, attachés, ambassadors—we never fail to turn up along with the salads, chickens, and desserts. The show must go on. It's called "A Message From Israel," though the MC makes sure to whisper in your ear that you should keep it down to fifteen minutes, because there are other speakers. "Give them a talk about 'The Situation.' "

However, my official representatives can't do all the

money machine's work. Most of this work, after all, does not take place at gala occasions. It's a gray, day-to-day business with lots of routine cultivation of small groups of people and individual contributors who demand personal attention. To meet these needs, you bring me to America on speaking tours.

Of course, you would prefer a cabinet minister, but if I'm a Knesset member, a journalist, an author, a businessman, or the like, you'll put up with me, too. It doesn't particularly matter if I'm famous, because you know that most of your clients have trouble remembering even the name of my prime minister, let alone, say, of my minister of the interior. You'll tell your audience I'm famous whether I am or not, and it won't matter in the least that no one has heard of me as long as I speak with an authentic Israeli accent.

Best of all, though, are the generals. You may be beginning to have your doubts about Israel, but you still can't help getting emotional at the sight of Jews who are soldiers, especially high-ranking ones. A general makes an excellent garnish not only at a UJA rally but even in your own homes. Comes the weekend you phone a few of your good friends and invite them out to your summer place for dinner or cocktails. "I've got someone really special for you—the commander who took Beirut!" Who can resist? Who can doubt the importance in the Jewish community of a man who hosts the general who (well, almost) took Beirut?

But whoever I am—general, Knesset member, author, or corporate executive—I follow the same route. You drag me from community to community, not leaving out the smallest or most forsaken place that has only a few dozen Jews, the oddest people with the oddest names. We pack in a full day—you know the routine better than I do.

The Leaders

Breakfast with "The Public Opinion Shapers Forum." Who exactly are the members of this forum? They include the local UJA chairman, a manufacturer of women's lingerie; the head of the federation, who deals in real estate; and the director of the Jewish Welfare Board, who happens to be a divorce lawyer. It's a representative sample of local Jews—but only of the go-getters who can and are willing to give a few thousand every year. The one exception is the rabbi. He's there to stand in for whatever money can't buy: spirituality, intellectualism, academic values, culture, and art. It's a tall order for one man to fill, and I find myself asking myself: Just who is the public whose opinion these men are supposed to shape?

The Statesmen

Mid-morning refreshments with "The International Relations Panel." On my way to meeting them the UJA chairman informs me that they're a highly serious group of people with a great interest in—what else?—international relations. I arrive to find some of them already waiting for me and some still drifting in. Their average age is between 65 and 80. While waiting for all eleven of these international experts to take their seats, my chairwoman engages me in small talk (naturally, about international relations) to keep me from being bored. "Whatever happened," she wants to know, "to that fellow, wait a minute, what's his name, oh, yes, Peres, Something-or-Other Peres, his first name's on the tip of my tongue. I've got it: Shamir! So tell me, what is Shamir Peres doing these days?"

The Fighters

For lunch I have some Second World War veterans. Their commanding officer is seated next to me. How do I know he's their commanding officer? Because when you, my escort, addressed him as "Mr. Chairman," he replied in a firm if trembling voice: "You can call me Colonel, sir, we have no chairmen around here." He's seated on my right, I am told, because he's hard of hearing in his left ear, from which a hearing aid is indeed dangling.

While eating my cold, tasteless chicken legs the Colonel tells me, not without considerable pride, that it's not enough to have been in the service during World War II to join his group—you have to have been stationed overseas. He also enlightens me about the difference between it and other groups of veterans. "They get together for parties, sporting events, go-go girls. We're more intellectual. Every month we meet for lunch and a lecture."

The Elders

Toward evening I'm brought to a building that is rather far out from the city. Stepping into it from the car, I'm overcome at once by the stale, stuffy air with its smells of diseases, medicines, and irreversible decline. A young black woman leads me to the office of this Jewish old age home. The news of my arrival has apparently caused no great sensation. This bitter truth is brought home to me by the shrill voice of my guide, who passes down the corridor calling out, "Great speaker tonight! Hey, we've got a great speaker tonight!"

On my way to the lecture hall I'm stopped several times with the eternal Jewish question, "Say, you wouldn't happen to know my cousin Joseph Goldstein in Netanya, would you?" A more original old lady pokes her cane at me and asks, "Are you the rabbi?" A middle-aged woman, the director of the UJA Senior Citizens Bureau, introduces me. "We have the great privilege," she announces, "of having for our speaker tonight the Israeli ambassador." I tug at her sleeve, but she shakes me off and continues to credit me with the ambassador's life and achievements.

As soon as my lecture is over, I turn to the chairwoman. "I'm not the ambassador," I protest, "and you know it." "My dear man," she answers with a shrug of forbearance, "these people gave up television, a card game, sleep, *something*, to come hear you. Don't you think they deserve at least an ambassador?"

(Indeed, I later found out that the ambassadorship awarded me was nothing compared to the titles given other Israelis. One, who as a young man was a low-ranking air force officer, was introduced as the father of the head of the air force. To be so he would have had to be at least twenty years older than his forty-seven years, but this minor discrepancy bothered no one. At another gathering the chairman was unhappy with the life history of the speaker, a professor of political science who had served as a lieutenant in the paratroopers. Looking for something more piquant, he asked his guest with pleading eyes, "Weren't you wounded in some war? Or maybe, God forbid, you lost a son in one?"

On the way back from the old age home I ask my escort what is the point of bringing speakers like me to such an institution in the first place. "But what do you mean, what's the point?" she asks back. "Those old people are sitting on millions!"

Meeting a group of millionaire elders, however, is good fun compared to a one-on-one session with one of them. Such was the fate of a speaker from Israel on whose schedule was written the name Rabinowitz. "Who's this Rabinowitz?" he inquired. "An important contributor who wants very much to meet you," was the answer. A UJA lady took the speaker on a two-hour drive to a home, where he was seated in an office. A few minutes later an old man the outline of whose diapers could be seen beneath his pants was brought in a wheelchair. He couldn't hear, he could hardly see, he couldn't speak. It turned out that he was over ninety. "What should I say to him?" the speaker asked. "Say to him," he was told, "that Israel is a good place that needs his money." Though our speaker did his best, he met with no sign of comprehension. "Israel good," screamed the UJA lady loudly into the old man's ear. "Israel very good." The old man's face remained expressionless as he was wheeled back out. "You've done a great mitzvah," the UJA lady told the speaker. "He'll give us lots of money."

Another speaker ended up mitzvah-less. He was brought by the local UJA executive to a hospital to visit an ailing old tycoon. The "Do Not Enter" sign on the door proved no obstacle. The executive pushed the door open and told the lecturer to follow him. The old man lay unconscious in bed, attached to a respirator. The UJA man took out a paper from his jacket pocket, a legal document leaving the UJA 25 thousand dollars from the dying man's estate. "Maybe he'll wake up and I can get him to sign," he explained to the speaker. "If necessary, you'll tell him you're from Israel and that you need the money badly. Just try to talk quickly."

The sick man did not awake, and after half-an-hour the Israeli speaker was obliged to go elsewhere. The UJA man phoned him that evening. "I'm sorry to say," he announced in a desolate voice, "that he died before I could get his signature."

The Israeli Corner

Later that evening there's a change of scenery. I'm driven to a suburb, which takes a very long time to get to. It's a quiet little town of some 300,000 inhabitants. I wonder, why would anyone want to live so far out?

Living far out and away from the racket, I am told, is everyone's dream. That's what brought people to the suburbs in the first place. The problem is that once they live there, they don't want to go back into the city for shopping and entertainment. And so shopping centers, restaurants, and movie houses follow them, and the racket they have fled from is back again. Now they have to move further out, to a suburb of the suburb. This time, too, they are loathe to return to their former neighborhood, and once again the sub-suburb fills up with shopping centers and restaurants. The racket is back again and they have to move again. Meanwhile, the old city center hardly has a shop left. The movie houses are gone from it, the office buildings stand empty. It's the quietest place in town.

I reach a low, sprawling condominium, a compound of

houses entered via a gate with a guard. It smells of fresh paint. In the race for tranquillity and status you mustn't stay put for more than a few years at a time. The houses are such that as soon as you step into one of them, you've seen them all. The same sofa, the same coffee table, the same armchairs, the same kitchen with its gadgets. Not to mention the same bathroom, with the same folded towels and the same little toylike bars of soap neatly arranged in the same little dish. So neatly arranged that it all seems to say, "Don't touch me, I'm only on display." (There's nothing I like better than taking one of these unused soap bars, lathering my hands well, opening a towel to dry them thoroughly, and flinging it down wet and crumpled alongside its prim sisters.)

The large living room is a sight for sore eyes. In it are several couples in their forties, although after the day I've had, they look much younger to me. According to the briefing I've been given, they are friends of Israel with whom I'm supposed to spend a quiet, informal evening. Despite their young age, however, their eyes, all eight pairs of them, are as tired as my own. And I haven't even opened my mouth yet! Not that I don't sympathize. I know they would rather be somewhere else just as I would. They're only here because it would have been impolite to refuse their host's invitation. Nevertheless, they all make an effort. As long as they're here, why not get the most of it? I'm asked about the political situation in Israel, the country's problems, the "Who Is A Jew?" debate, until at last, inevitably, comes the searching question: "How will it all end?"

It all ends with coffee and cake. For everyone except

me. Because there is something that I must, simply must, see. With a proud smile my host steers me to the far corner of the living room, which is his Israeli corner. There I find everything that a genuine Israelophile should have. In the middle is a large photograph of my host with the Israeli prime minister. If the host is very important, that is, very wealthy, he's shaking hands with him. If he's less important, that is, less wealthy, there are three or four other people with him. And so it goes. Some have to settle for the third row of a group photograph among dozens of people—or, if they're even more ordinary than that, to make do with a mere general or Knesset member.

All around the big photograph are smaller photographs. A picture of the Israeli plaque: "This room (or building) is a donation of the Harry Cohen family of Baltimore." A picture of the family at Masada (a must). A picture with an Arab holding a camel (another must). Assorted pictures taken at the Sea of Galilee, in Elath, in Tel Aviv (optional).

Above the photographs is a bookshelf. A book about politics, a book about American Jewry, a book about Masada (all optional). But the mustest must is Abba Eban. *My People, My Land*—it doesn't matter what else there is, an Israeli corner without Abba Eban's history is like the United States without the Declaration of Independence.

By the side of the photographs is the bric-a-brac. A Hanukkah menorah—that's obvious—in which are embedded a few small stones that the shopowner claimed came from the Wailing Wall, although they could just as well be from Korea. An ashtray from Safed (quite possibly also from Korea). A keychain with "Shalom" in Hebrew letters. A *hamsa* or an antique-looking jug. It's important to have *something* from the Arab market in Jerusalem, right? That's Israel too, after all, and it's so exotic. And of course, it was a steal. For the umpteenth time I hear the story of how the Arab wanted $250 for it, but my host said 10 ("Ten?" gasps your audience while he explains knowledgeably that that's the only way to bargain), and the Arab said 175, but when my host turned to walk away, he came down to 45. "A steal," murmurs everyone in agreement. (The piece, of course, was worth four dollars, five at the most.)

The finishing touches of the corner are the modestly hung certificates. A certificate of honor for work in the Jewish community and for Israel. Man of the Year. Man of the Decade. Man of the Century.

The wife has been thought of, too. The operators of the money machine are well aware of her potential and have come up with something special for her: a Bride of Israel marriage document. In return for so many dollars, we are informed, she has been lawfully married to the state of Israel and the Jewish people. For a different sum she would have received a statue of a lion by a "famous" sculptor, symbolizing her membership in the elite "Lions of Judah." This lion has holes in it. With every fresh contribution a precious or semi-precious stone is set in one of them, according to the size of the pledge. Both the lion and the marriage document, needless to say, have a place of honor in the corner. No one is left out.

If I think that my tour of the Israeli corner has earned me my cake and coffee, I have another guess coming. Now I am called upon to settle a dispute as to whether the Golan Heights are pronounced "GOH-len" or "Go-

LAHN." Why is it important? Because my interlocutor has a cousin in Beersheba, which is near the Golan Heights, isn't it? As a matter of fact, perhaps I know her. Just when I get a piece of cake into my mouth I have to hear the story of a proud father whose daughter has traveled to Russia. "I spoke again with her on the phone today—boy, I'm going to get some bill!" Next comes the story of the son whose mother watched Sadat's visit to Jerusalem on TV in Los Angeles and phoned him at once to say, "Did you see Sadat and Begin shaking hands? Who would have believed it? Only in America!"

Sunday is a day off in America. Not for a speaker from Israel, though. That's the day he's dragged off to Sunday School, that horrid invention whose traumatic impact will accompany you and your children till the day you die. And as if it isn't bad enough that they have to learn Hebrew while their friends are out playing baseball or football, today they have to listen to some man tell them stories about a country called Israel. The little eyes facing me range from indifference to hostility. I don't blame them. Is this your way of teaching them that being a Jew is no picnic?

JUDAH: I've listened to you with great patience. I gather from your descriptions that I seem ridiculous and absurd to you. But why do you talk about it so angrily, almost hatefully? What upsets you so much?

ISRAEL: Just a minute. Before I answer you, I have to correct a false impression I may have given. A lecture tour in America isn't always an exhausting obstacle course. Sometimes you run into an organization that it's a pleasure to appear before.

JUDAH: Really? I'm very pleased to hear that.

ISRAEL: Like a certain organization located in a medium-sized city in Middle America. It's members—

JUDAH: But what's it called? Why all the secrecy?

ISRAEL: You'll see in a minute. The all-male members of this organization get together once a month for dinner and a lecture. Their meetings are held in a hotel. Always. At one such meeting the lecturer was from Israel and he was going great guns about The Situation. Despite his virtuoso rhetorical powers, however, he could feel his audience growing impatient. The men fidgeted in their chairs, glanced at their watches, exchanged whispers. Only when he was through did he understand why. The dinner and the lecture, explained the beaming chairman, were not the only items on the monthly agenda. Still to come was the pièce de résistance, which, with no disrespect intended to Israel, was a prostitute waiting in one of the hotel rooms to give the men their jollies.

The procedure was as follows: Whoever wished to enjoy the lady's favors anted up thirty or forty dollars and a name was drawn from a hat. The winner got the whore for free and the whore got the kitty. On this occasion, however, the speaker from Israel was awarded the prize as a special gesture without having to compete in the raffle.

What hospitality! It left everyone happy, the speaker, the prostitute, the group members, and even their wives, who were proud of their husbands' sacrificing their beauty sleep for an intellectual cause. But I'm sorry . . . the story made me forget what your question was.

JUDAH: Me too. No, I remember. You talk about the

things that I do with absolute rage. Why? Why do they bother you so much?

ISRAEL: I'll tell you why. When my speaking tour was over, I found myself sitting in the airport one day waiting for my return flight to Israel. I thought of my meetings with the public opinion shapers, the international relations experts, the Second World War veterans, the sub-suburbanites, the elders of the old age home, and the Sunday School children, and I asked myself, "What on earth have I—the general, the executive, the senior government official, the Knesset member, or the author—been doing here?"

Just then I thought of a little Turkish town on the Black Sea called Antalya. It's a lovely spot—old houses, winding lanes, a colorful square by the harbor with cafes and peddlers trying to earn a few pennies from the tourists. The main attraction was a man with a trained bear on a chain. Now and then he would stop by some tourists and the bear would do a few tricks for which he was rewarded with a piece of meat, after which his master went around collecting coins in a copper plate.

After my tour of America, I felt like that bear.

JUDAH: But this is absurd! Do I bring you to America on a chain? Why do you come if that's how you feel?

ISRAEL: Why does the bear do his tricks? For the piece of meat he gets from his master. The fact is, however, that I'm worse than the poor bear. He needs the meat to stay alive, whereas I perform for a free trip. Like almost every Israeli I'm dying to go abroad, to get away from it all for at least a few days—from the claustrophobia, the *Intifada,* the siege of millions of Arabs, the taxes, the mutual intolerance, the pettiness. I want to breathe the air of open spaces, of countries where there is no PLO and no Israelis. Don't get me wrong. Of course, I tell myself and others that I'm doing it to help out, that it's a way to put my shoulder to the wheel by collecting money for my people and my country. But the quite wretched reality is that I do it for the free ticket, the hotel expenses, and the pocket money. That's my piece of meat, for which I'm willing not only to be dragged to every small town and old age home, but to say exactly what you want me to say. For it I'll parrot every one of the beloved clichés that you never tire of hearing. The best one to lead off a lecture with is "Israel will live forever." It's always good for a big round of applause that puts a twinkle in the eye of every speaker and UJA chairman. Next comes a seven or eight minute review of the current situation in Israel. It doesn't matter what's in it as long as you don't forget to declare, "It will never happen again!" That's an even bigger applause-getter. You don't have to explain what "It" refers to: every Jewish child—or at least every Jewish child who has ever attended a UJA rally—knows it's the Holocaust. For the clincher—an indispensable line if you want your chairman to remember you kindly and invite you back again next year—you always wind up with, "We in Israel know that we can depend on you—we are one people!" There's no better way to become your chairman's darling and automatically be labeled "a stimulating speaker."

Anything but the most superficial remarks about subjects like Zionism or Jewish identity are a disaster. Any non-cliché is dangerous and unwise. Within a few minutes your audience is so bleary-eyed that only a hastily shouted

"Israel will live forever!" can save the situation. Unless, that is, the yawns have already begun, in which case you may have to add without waiting, "It will never happen again!" The one-people routine, however, should always be saved for the end.

The one thing that must be avoided at all costs is to say what you really think. Anyone insane enough to commit such a faux pas should know that it's his last visit in UJA-land. Apart from which, it's a sheer waste of breath. All that will happen is that you will be told that you were "controversial," which is a polite word for good-bye. Nothing is more loathed by a UJA chairman than a controversial Israeli speaker.

In short: If you want another ticket (and I have yet to meet the Israeli who didn't) make sure you're stimulating but not controversial.

No UJA chairperson automatically assumes that his speaker knows the rules of the game. On the way from the airport to your hotel, therefore, your chairperson will want to know what you think about the subjects you're speaking on. "That's very, very interesting," you'll be told if you happen to think the wrong things, "but you have to understand that our point of view over here is different and you're liable to leave people with the wrong impression and hurt their feelings." Usually the speaker gets the hint and everything goes smoothly.

What happens, though, if he doesn't? What happens is what happened to me on my last visit to America in 1989, before Gorbachev opened the floodgates. At the end of one of my talks I was asked about your "Passage To Freedom" campaign and I expressed my opinion that it was bad for Israel and Zionism because it encouraged Soviet Jews to settle in America rather than in Israel. The next morning I received a telephone from your national chairman—or maybe it was your vice president, I have trouble keeping all those titles straight—in which he spoke rather loudly. "What the hell did you think you were doing?" he wanted to know. "You ruined the local campaign!" I had the right to my opinions, he went on, but I was not there to express them. I was there to help raise money. If I was against the campaign, I should never have come.

JUDAH: Don't you think he was right?

ISRAEL: I think he was as right as could be.

JUDAH: So what did you do?

ISRAEL: I laid off the subject.

JUDAH: Because he was right?

ISRAEL: Because I didn't want to burn my golden bridges to America. Because I wanted him to invite me back.

JUDAH: But you resent us because of it!

ISRAEL: No. I don't feel resentment. I feel sorry for both of us. For you because you think you need me, and for me because, for a few goodies, I'm willing to be your clown.

PIECE OF ISRAEL

ISRAEL: I don't play the clown only when I visit you. I play it in Israel when you visit me, too. I'm willing to turn any truck that will please you and make you feel that you've gotten your money's worth. I even serve up my country's leaders to you. To you, Mr. Fabrics Dealer, to you, Mr. Underwear Manufacturer . . .

89

JUDAH: Or Mr. Lawyer, or Mr. Doctor, or Mr. Musician . . .

ISRAEL: Those are types that generally don't go in for all this, but let's not quibble. Whoever you are, I'll serve you up a great tour. I'll take you to kibbutzim, to universities, to big cities, and little development towns. I'll bring you to army and air force bases, where my generals will give you a briefing on the military lineup in the area. They'll show you their tanks, their artillery pieces, their airplanes. Now you're not only a statesman, you're a military strategist, too. And you let my generals know it with your questions. How high can that plane over there fly? How much time does it need to reach Damascus? Can we deter the Syrians with it?

We. Us. Ours. You've bought yourself a whole army. A whole country. For less than 1 percent of your yearly income. Tax-deductible.

And your tour isn't over yet. The guns, the tanks, the planes, the kibbutzim, the universities—I let you see them to show you that your money isn't wasted, that it's been invested wisely and well. Needless to say, that makes you happy and proud. But it isn't enough. It's . . . well . . . kind of general. After all, you're not just a representative of American Jewry, you're *you*, Harry, Steve, or Marvin. And you want something more specific to show what *your* money went for.

In a word: You want a plaque.

Since we wouldn't dream of making you unhappy we've established the biggest and best plaque industry in the world. It's not that you're unfamiliar with the saying that the highest form of philanthropy is anonymous, it's just that you don't think that it was meant for you. That's why

I see your name everywhere. In my hospitals, my universities, my army, my playing fields, my government offices. "This Building Was Built With The Generous Donation of Harry and Barbara Levy Los Angeles, California." I can't deny that a sign like that is a bargain—to get an entire building for so few words is definitely a good price. In most cases, though, the size of the plaque varies in inverse proportion to the donation. "This Garden Was Donated By Steven and Esther Shapiro of Cheyenne, Wyoming, In Loving Memory of Their Parents Zelda, Jacob, Martha, and Isaac, and in the Name of Their Children Dorothy, Henry, Hilda, and Stanley." The whole garden is five by ten feet and comprises one rose bush and two flowerbeds. The Shapiros, it would seem, could not even afford a bit of grass.

And if a whole building or even a garden is beyond your means, don't worry: You can still plant a tree in the Holy Land. Or even a grove, forest, or jungle. Whatever suits you best. We'll bring you there, and on the trunk of your tree, or at the entrance of your forest, grove, or jungle, you'll find your name and the names of your wife, parents, children, or anyone else you wish to list as a codonor in gold lettering on a black background. What bliss it is to own a piece of your ancestral homeland! And, of course, you haven't left your camera behind. As soon as you get home you'll have the photograph enlarged and framed, and you'll stand it in your Israeli corner.

After taking a few pictures, you climb back on your bus and drive off. But the caretaker of your grove or forest stays behind. It's his job to change the plaque for the next donor.

After all, we have a small country. How many trees can I plant in it? It's easier and more profitable to change the plaque.

And anyhow, you couldn't care less. Once I accompanied a group of donors from Philadelphia. One of the things they were supposed to do was to plant some trees in a forest near Jerusalem. On the way to the tree planting the driver stopped for gas. It began to rain. When the driver started up the bus again, grumbles were heard from the group. One of them, a dentist in his early forties, told our tour guide that there was "no way" they were going to plant trees in the rain. Our guide was experienced enough to take it in stride and come up with an instant solution. "No problem," he told the group. "We'll get off the bus and plant a symbolic tree here, by the roadside. I'll see to it that it's transferred later on to the forest and that the rest of the trees are planted alongside it with the plaque." Everybody was happy.

What am I getting at? That the group members didn't love the soil of the Holy Land? That their greatest wish was not to leave some trace of themselves in it? Perish the thought! But that still didn't mean they had to get wet. And if that meant winking at the white lie that their tree would be moved to the forest, they were perfectly happy to wink.

JUDAH: Maybe they believed the guide would really keep his promise.

ISRAEL: I'd rather not think they were so naive. They simply couldn't have cared less. All they wanted was to get back to their warm, cozy hotel rooms. They didn't give a damn where some poor little sapling would stand.

It's just a game. The donation is for the plaque. If it were really for the tree, after all, the plaque could be dispensed with. And Israelis can plant their own trees if they need them. We play the game because it feeds the money machine. You get what you want and I get what I want. We're both happy. Which is, of course, the problem. Because each of us should feel humiliated, embarrassed. Instead, we're both pleased as punch.

Almost. Because one thing is still missing. So far I've showed you what I've done with your money, but that isn't enough. It can even be counterproductive, because you may make the terrible mistake of thinking that everything is fine and dandy with me. I have guns, I have tanks, I have airplanes, I have hospitals, I have universities, I have trees—but if I have so much, perhaps I don't need your money anymore or need less of it? You mustn't be left with that fatal impression. You must—so I'm told by your money-machine leaders—you must go back to America feeling that your work is still cut out for you. Which is why I bring you—at the very end of your trip, so that you'll remember it best—to the other side of the tracks, to the urban slums and poor development towns that dot the country. They never fail to make the desired impression, as their inhabitants are the first to realize.

A whole folklore has sprung up around these visits, from which the following story, I assume, derives. It is said that the head of a local neighborhood council once came to the ministry of finance to demand a special budget for his constituency. Pounding on the desk, he declared: "I'm not asking for favors! We're a good business. You bring us UJA delegations and we tell them how awful our lives are.

We purposely keep our neighborhood rundown for them to see how poor we are. We bring in lots of dollars and we want our share of them." If the special budget was granted, he promised, not a penny of it would be used to upgrade the appearance of the neighborhood.

JUDAH: It sounds apocryphal to me.

ISRAEL: No doubt it is. But it still says something about how I see the way you see me.

Those poor, unfortunate Israelis: How you love us that way! I'm reminded of a stop once made by one of our Israeli speakers. It was in a suburb of Los Angeles. Not an ordinary suburb either, but someplace really exclusive. The minute the speaker arrived he realized that he was in one of the poshest neighborhoods in town, though a very non-Californian one. What was special about it was its understatement. The red-roofed houses were not particularly large and there was an almost pastoral quiet. Pastoral quiet, however, was not the host's idea of good taste. It didn't go with making it big. And so he had torn down the original house and built in its place a replica of the Taj Mahal, complete with a wishing fountain.

It was mid-day and a luncheon was being given by a woman's group to which the hostess belonged. Taj Mahal or not, there was no mistaking the scene for India. On the roof stood a thin, bearded young man dressed in rags, an old cap on his head and—what else?—a violin in one hand, playing numbers from *Fiddler On The Roof.* Tevya comes to the Taj Mahal. Boiberik in Los Angeles.

At a table by the front door sat an extremely well-groomed woman of about sixty, handing out brochures with a gracious smile. In them was an illustrated account of the neighborhood renewal project in Israel that the ladies had gathered to discuss. Musrara. A slum in Jerusalem.

Brochures in hand, the ladies and the speaker were taken on a tour of the house, the worth of whose contents could have solved most of Musrara's problems. The walls, buffets, closets, everything, were made of green jade brought specially from China. On the walls hung a Manet, a Gauguin, a Van Gogh. There was no end of exotically glittering rooms.

Finally, the ladies sat down to hear about the project they had clasped to their generous bosoms. When the speaker was done describing it, his hostess rose and announced with a lump in her throat that the hard lives of the unfortunate residents of Musrara broke her heart. And so—especially since she was hosting the occasion and had to serve as an example—she had decided to pledge . . . $800. Eight hundred! Far less than the cost of one of the picture frames on her walls. Far, far less than the cost of the chair the speaker was sitting on. And no less teary-eyed, all the other ladies rose and announced their pledges after her: $600, $500, $550. Slightly more or less than they had spent on their hairdressers before coming to hear about Musrara. After all, you wouldn't dream of visiting the Taj Mahal without first renewing your permanent!

What good does it do? It's not only an embarrassment, it's no longer even relevant. No doubt it served a purpose during the first decade or two of Israel's existence, but you've kept it up long after it stopped making sense. At every gathering, at every get-together: What poor unfortunates are you talking about? It's true that not every

Israeli owns the Taj Mahal, but your average Israeli does drive a Cadillac and lives in a luxury villa. How is that? A medium-size car in Israel costs $25,000, which is more or less what a Cadillac will run you, and the roads are full of such cars; a small five-room apartment in Tel Aviv goes for $300,000, and such apartments are snapped up the minute they go on the market; every summer half-a-million Israelis, that is to say, 15 percent of the country's population, go on vacations abroad. Imagine 35 million Americans doing that!

JUDAH: And what is Musrara, a wealthy suburb?

ISRAEL: Of course we have poor people. Is there a country that doesn't? It's just that my poor are better off than your poor. None of them is starving, because I don't allow that to happen.

So what's so unfortunate about me? I realize that it's easier to raise money for someone who is depicted that way, but don't you realize that you demean me? That you turn me into a failure? And maybe that's just the point. Maybe you *like* thinking I'm a failure, so that you can think, "It's no accident that all the successful Jews are here and all the welfare cases are there." And it's not at all a bad alibi for not coming to live in Israel yourself—but that's something I won't get into just yet.

A poor, unfortunate clown: That's what you've turned me into. And a grasping one, too. Money and Israel are one and the same thing for you. You peddle the lie to your Jews that they are partners in my country, that without them I would almost certainly go bankrupt. Is it any wonder that our president and prime minister and minister of tourism receive thousands of letters from you like the one that read, "When I was in Jerusalem I bought a necklace for 30 dollars, but at the airport on my way home I saw the same necklace for 20 dollars. Last year I contributed 300 dollars to UJA. If you don't return my 10 dollars to me, I'll never contribute again. Sincerely Yours, etc."?

Nothing is too sacred for the money machine. Jerusalem, the Wailing Wall, Auschwitz, my human and national dignity.

Even my blood.

That's just more grist for the mill. Is there a war on in Lebanon? A terrorist attack? Right from the airport you and your delegation are brought straight to the hospital to see the wounded. And, of course, only the most serious cases, the amputees, after which you're told how vital it is to up your pledge for the sake of these wonderful young fighting men. The more limbs lost, the more money.

JUDAH: It's you who take me to see them. I don't go barging into hospitals uninvited.

ISRAEL: I've already said I'm no better than you in this respect. I'm as much in thrall to the money machine as you are. I give you whatever you ask for. You want slums? Coming right up. Just tell me if you want an urban slum or a rural slum, a slum in Tel Aviv or a slum in the sticks. You want wounded soldiers? No problem. Just let me know how you want them: freshly wounded or convalesced, nonambulatory or blind—don't be embarrassed to ask, I've got a wide selection. And for dessert there's always the president, the prime minister, a Knesset member, or a general. We try to please.

I give you things I can't even get myself. It doesn't matter how much taxes I pay or how many limbs I and my family have lost in this or that war. If I'm an average Israeli my chances of meeting the chief-of-staff aren't much greater than of winning the national lottery. The situation isn't hopeless, though: I only have to pack up and leave for America myself. Once I've made some money there, I can contribute a few thousand dollars to the cause and come to Israel on a UJA mission. Then every door will be open. I'll be smiled at, stroked, told how much I'm doing for Israel.

Do you understand what's happening here? I spend three years in the army, I'm in the reserves for most of my life, I may lose an arm or a son in action, half of my income goes to taxes—and my leaders tell me that if I want to be somebody, I have to live in America and pledge a few hundred or thousand dollars every year, part of which is tax—

JUDAH: . . . deductible. Yes, you've already made your point.

ISRAEL: And just in case the president, the prime minister, a well-known author, a prominent journalist, a distinguished general, a Knesset member, and some slums aren't enough to do the trick, don't hesitate to tell me, I've got a tour for you that no Jewish pocket can resist. The ultimate.

It's starts with the Holocaust Memorial in Jerusalem. Death camps. Gas chambers. Children's corpses. Piles of shoes and human teeth. Factories for Jewish soap. There won't be a dry eye, I promise you. The most tightly zipped pocket will show signs of opening.

But wait, I'm not through. Nearby I've got the straw that will break the battered camel's back. Because out of the ashes rose a Jewish state to make sure it doesn't happen again—and it too has its fallen. The military cemetery on Mount Herzl: I'll give your victims an unforgettable tour of it. Oh, I know, I know: After all, I've gotten to know you. A tour is fine, but it's not enough. I need a gimmick, too. The gimmick's the thing, and it has to be specific. The graves of a whole lot of dead young men are impressive but kind of general. What you want is a story. A story you can tell to your friends. And I happen to have just the thing for you. A grave your victims will be wild about. There's not a delegation that isn't.

Several hours ahead of time, I send my tour guide to cover the grave of the deceased. When your group arrives, the guide tells you how hard it is to be an Israeli parent sending his or her son off to war. He tells about the conflicts, the anxieties, the fear of picking up the telephone when it rings late at night. And then, when your victims' eyes are already wet, *then,* in a low but dramatic voice, your guide asks one of you to uncover the grave. An inscription is revealed. Slowly your victims take it in. KILLED IN THE WAR OF INDEPENDENCE. BY AN ARAB SNIPER. IN JERUSALEM. WHILE CARRYING MESSAGES BETWEEN POSITIONS. And the kicker: AGE THIRTEEN. That does it. Everyone is thinking of his Stevie or Brian who just celebrated their bar-mitzvah. You needn't say another word. The message is clear: Just think of the price Israelis must pay and of how lucky you are to be in America . . . and then, please reach for your checkbook!

And we lament that Israelis want to emigrate, that they want to assimilate! Why shouldn't they? Who wants to be identified with a country that always has its hand in your pocket and whose ultimate value, to which everything else is subordinated, is money? Why would anyone want to belong to it and to such a people?

JUDAH: I can only say again that I fail to see why you're coming to me with all this. I couldn't do a fraction of the things you describe if you refused to cooperate.

ISRAEL: If my leaders refused to cooperate. That's true, just as it's true that it's pointless to expect them to stop this disgraceful state of affairs. That's why it will only be stopped by you when you no longer want me as your clown. And here there's room for hope.

JUDAH: Why is that?

ISRAEL: Because you're beginning to view me as more of a burden than an asset. You're sore at me. How could the same people who brought you the Six Day War and Entebbe now bring you the War in Lebanon and the Pollard case? I'm tarnishing your image. And what's more, I'm fouling up your money machine.

The *Intifada* has made it much worse. On my last visit to you one of your machinists complained to me that he was in a fix. "Every year I'm expected to raise more funds, but every year your image hits a new low, and with it, our contributions."

The truth of this was brought home to me this time,

when, after my first speech, a pleasant-looking middle-aged Jew came up to me and said angrily: "I'm not giving Israel any more money because of the way it treats the Palestinians." And it's not just your rank-and-file that's up in arms. Your officer corps is beginning to grumble, too. So far it's still in a whisper, like that of the federation president in a small Middle-Western city who turned to me over our bagels-and-lox and said, "Maybe you can help me out of my dilemma. I give a lot of money—" (afterwards I was told that he was the biggest pledger in the area, which of course was why he was president) "—and I'm starting to think that I'm giving it to a government whose policies are a disaster. What do you suggest I do?" I looked him in his anguished eyes. "Don't worry," I whispered back, "most of the money you raise stays right here in your community." His eyes lit up. "You know something?" he said. "I never thought of that."

That's my great hope. That one day you'll decide that you have no more use for me and leave me alone. You won't want me as your clown or your basket case anymore. And you won't let sentiment stand in your way. The minute you decide that I'm no good for the money machine—that in fact, I'm bad for it—you won't hesitate to tell me good-bye and good riddance.

JUDAH: But until that happens, if it ever does, what do you suggest we do? Stop giving you money?

ISRAEL: Of course. I've already said it isn't worth it. The moral damage is far greater than the financial benefit. After all, what's at stake? Everything you give me barely comes to 2 percent of my annual budget. All the hocus-pocus, all the humiliation, all the disgrace—for barely 2 percent of my budget!

JUDAH: But it isn't just the money. I really do want to identify with you somehow. Even if you aren't interested, even if it disturbs you, it's important to me that we do something together. For all the system's faults, I'd rather have Jews who identify with Israel than Jews who don't. Today those Jews identify by giving money. Do you have an alternative?

ISRAEL: Investment. Don't give me charity. If you want an involvement with Israel, go right ahead: take your money and invest it there.

JUDAH: What makes you prefer that?

ISRAEL: First of all, it's more respectable. It's your money and I want you to get a good return for it on a purely financial basis. Without favors or slogans or plaques. And secondly, from a Zionist point of view it's more efficient. You're an odd fellow, you know. Once you give a contribution you don't really care what happens to it. All that matters to you is your plaque. You'd like to think that your money is serving some useful purpose, but you're not going to lose any sleep over it. When you invest your money, though, it's another story. You're a businessman. A bad investment makes you a failure to yourself and to your friends. Worse than that, it makes you a sucker. If you invest in Israel, you'll do everything you can to make sure that your investment pays off. You'll call on your experience and expertise. You'll send a few of your managers over here. You may even send one of your children to run the business, just as the Canadian Murray Koffler did with Superpharm. We'll profit not just from your money but from your know-how, and as an extra bonus, maybe some of the people you send over, maybe even one of your own children, will settle here for good. Another extra will be that you'll have more respect for us, just as we will have for you.

JUDAH: I've already tried it. I've come to Israel all eager to invest, and what happened? Everywhere I ran into bureaucracy, an endless obstacle course of permits and officials.

ISRAEL: And so you said to yourself, "To hell with it, what do I need this headache for, I'll give my contribution every year and I'll be left in peace." Yes, I know what you're talking about. But honestly, it wasn't just the bureaucracy, was it? Are there really no bureaucrats in America? There are in fact some pretty bad ones, but you've learned to put up with them and you don't give up until you get what you want from them. It's only in Israel that you take no for an answer right away.

We're back in our vicious circle again: You won't invest in Israel because of our bureaucracy, and our bureaucracy is what it is because you won't invest.

JUDAH: What does one thing have to do with the other?

ISRAEL: A great deal. If you were really determined to invest, if you gave us a choice of either your investment or nothing, we would simplify our bureaucratic procedures. We would have to. You would force us to. But if you throw in the towel before you've even begun to fight, what wonder is it that the bureaucracy wins?

JUDAH: I have my hands full running my business in America. Do you really think I have the time and strength to fight a war with your bureaucrats in Israel?

103

ISRAEL: I'm quite sure you would find the time and strength if the option of philanthropy were denied you. I believe that you feel the need for an involvement with Israel for all the reasons we've spoken of. As long as you can do that philanthropically, you'll prefer to. It's easier. It's less of a nuisance. But that's precisely why we shouldn't let you get away with it. If you need charity campaigns for your own communal needs—go right ahead and run them. Just keep us out of it.

JUDAH: But how, practically speaking, would it work? Of course, if I have a million or two to invest, there's no problem. But what about the small givers, those who contribute a few hundred dollars a year? Aren't you leaving them out in the cold?

ISRAEL: By no means. The approach I'm calling for would turn the UJA and bonds offices into investment centers. Shares would be offered in different enterprises and anyone could buy as many or as few of them as he wished. In fact, I should think that people with low or median incomes would be more attracted to investment. It's harder for them to give a few hundred dollars of charity than it is for Bronfman to give his millions. I'm sure they would much prefer to own part of some business in return for their money.

JUDAH: I can see how investment would be a better solution for you. It might be a better one for me too if only the UJA—the money machine, as you call it—were solely a matter of raising funds. But that isn't the case. You yourself have said, and I heartily agree, that UJA campaigns have become a focus of Jewish activity. In fact, they're the glue that holds Jewish life in America together. And it's no accident that they revolve around you. For all your problems and faults, you're still the one thing that Jews everywhere can identify with. Orthodox, Reform, Conservative, secular—you're the only issue they can all unite on. That's why I need the UJA, and I need to build it around you. It's a full-time job to preserve Jewish identity in America.

ISRAEL: You're wasting your time. I might be willing to go on playing the clown for you if I thought there was a chance, even a slim one, of its helping. But I'm convinced that the opposite is true. I'm absolutely convinced that the path you're taking leads nowhere—or to put it differently, to extinction. Both yours and mine. Because this path allows us to ignore the fact that I am now too tired and weak to preserve Israel and you are too comfortable and well-padded to be able to preserve your Judaism.

JUDAH: Do you know of a better one?

ISRAEL: I know of only one possibilty.

JUDAH: I'm listening.

ISRAEL: It's not anything you'll want to hear, believe me.

JUDAH: What makes you say that?

ISRAEL: Everything you tell me. A few months ago I was asked to speak to a group of yours that had finished a tour in Israel. It was their first visit here. Before I began, their tour guide gave me some instructions. The first was to say, "Coming to Israel takes courage. You did it and you should feel proud of yourselves." The second was, "Explain to them that the Hebrew word for charity, *tsedakah,* comes from the word *tsedek,* which means justice." The fourth was, "Tell them that if they stop giving or give less than the maximum, all kinds of things, such as immigrant absorption, will grind to a halt."

JUDAH: You left out the third.

ISRAEL: That's because it's the thing you don't want to hear. That you won't allow me to talk about.

JUDAH: Try me.

ISRAEL: The third instruction given me was, "Make sure you don't mention aliyah."*

* The Hebrew word for immigration of Jews to Israel.

3

The Unmentionable Choice
for American Jews:
Assimilate or Emigrate

JUDAH: I doubt very much whether there is any use in discussing the possibility of significant immigration of American Jews to Israel. Don't you think it's pointless?

ISRAEL: That depends. If we're talking about you and me in general, as Jews, I think there is. In fact, I think there's no point in discussing anything else. Everything else is marginal, unimportant. We've made an art of talking about everything in the world apart from the one thing that matters most of all: our survival, yours and mine.

If we're talking about us as individual Israelis and Jews, on the other hand, I agree that we have a problem. I'm not insensitive. I realize that it's far from simple for a man to give up a good career, a big house, an expensive car, and a country that's pleasant to live in and exchange it one day for a strange land with a strange language and a strange way of thinking and doing things. I want you to understand that I know just how hard, how almost inhuman, that is. So if you tell me that's it, that you don't want to live in Israel because you're content in America, period, I'll leave you in peace and we can consider our conversation finished. Is it?

JUDAH: It is. But there are other reasons, too.

ISRAEL: I knew you'd say that. And it's those other reasons that infuriate me. They make me madder than the fact of your not living here. Because they're the crux of the vicious circle, and the conspiracy of silence radiates out from them.

But all right, let's hear them, those other reasons of yours.

JUDAH: What have you done to give me the feeling that my place as a Jew is with you? Why, you've done just the opposite! You've turned your country into a secular, almost atheistical state. I never expected you to keep all the commandments, but that doesn't mean you can't keep any of them. You don't know what the inside of a synagogue looks like. You travel on the Sabbath. You eat pork as if it were just another food. You spend the most important Jewish holidays in places of entertainment. There's nothing Jewish about you or your life—and you expect me to live in Israel because I'm a Jew?

ISRAEL: Who says that Jewishness is a matter of going to synagogue and not eating pork? I don't need to go to synagogue to feel Jewish. I don't have to spend Yom Kippur fasting and praying, because Yom Kippur and Rosh Hashanah and all the other Jewish holidays are national days of rest and not just religious occasions. It's enough for me to open my eyes in the morning to know that it's Yom Kippur or Rosh Hashanah.

You need the symbolism of the synagogue to feel Jewish. If you didn't attend it on Yom Kippur you wouldn't know or feel what day it is, because nothing around you would look any different. Your holidays aren't your country's. If I ever disappear as a Jew it won't be because of the things you list but because when I cease to be a majority, a majority I don't belong to determines the ambience in which I live. Which brings us to the first link in the tragic, vicious circle in which our relationship revolves. Ultimately, if you don't come live with me, I will cease to be a majority. And that's when I'll start attending synagogue and eating kosher food to feel Jewish. Will I be more of a Jew then? Will the day I'm a synagogue-going minority be the day you'll come to live with me? Do I have to stop being the master of my own house and become like you before I can be worthy of you?

Honestly now: Is that really the problem? Is that the real reason you don't live in Israel?

JUDAH: I'm not sure. But I do know that there's very little about you that attracts me.

ISRAEL: I'm afraid that by the time you realize that the issue isn't whether I attract you, not only will you have disappeared, I will have too.

JUDAH: I've been hearing about Jewish people's disappearance for the past two thousand years. If Antiochus and Hitler couldn't make us disappear, you'll excuse me for not being worried.

ISRAEL: I may excuse you, but I can't agree with you. Antiochus and Hitler failed, that's true. So did the Inquisition. So did everyone who set out to destroy the Jewish people. But do you know why they did? It's not because we're immortal. It's because they chose the wrong tactic. They didn't understand that you can't destroy the Jews by violence. The more the Gentiles hate us, discriminate against us, attack us physically, the more sophisticated our defense mechanisms become.

No. The Jewish people can cope with anti-Semitism. The one thing it can't cope with is philo-Semitism.

Which is what you have today in the United States. And if it's not active philo-Semitism, it's at least the absence of active anti-Semitism. You have a free society that allows you to be yourselves with almost no discrimination. And faced with it, you're helpless.

111

JUDAH: If you're trying to tell me that there is no more anti-Semitism in America, I have news for you.

ISRAEL: I know what there is in America. On my last speaking tour I was warned by one of your money machine operators: "Be careful what you say, because there may be non-Jews in the audience." In different places I was told how non-Jews had ways of putting Jews in their place. Not in so many words. Snidely. Like the Rotary luncheon at which the chairman asked different tables different questions until he came to a table with two Jews at it and said, "The question I have for you is of a tribal nature."

Or like the argument between the Jewish and the non-Jewish woman over which of them should ask a Jewish holdout for a contribution to some local charity. After summing up all her reasons the non-Jew said, "But you'll do better than me, it's in your blood." Meaning, of course: No one cadges money like a Jew.

Or like the woman who drove me back to my hotel and told me on our way that her twenty-seven-year-old son worked for a big automobile company in Detroit. Did he like his job? I asked. Not so much, was the answer, because after four or five years he had yet to be promoted. "I don't want to sound paranoid," she continued hesitantly, "but I think it's because he's Jewish." There may have been other reasons for her son's stalled career, and as a Jewish mother she may have preferred to think he was a victim of anti-Semitism rather than of his own lack of ability. Certainly, though, the word "anti-Semitism" has not disappeared from the American Jewish vocabulary.

But I think you use it inaccurately. You say "anti-

Semitism" when what you actually mean is ethnic stereo-typing. True, you may still feel uncomfortable or an outsider in the company of non-Jews, just as they may feel in yours, even if this feeling is on the decline and no longer exists in many groups and places. One way or another, your Jewishness can be a barrier even in the most unprejudiced circles. You're constantly doing your best to be just like other Americans, but being just like other Americans for a Jew is like being half-pregnant for a woman. In order to really be like them you would have to stop being Jewish. They can open their golf clubs to you and let you up to the top floors of their banks, but as Christians they can never accept you unreservedly, because Judaism, as the Protestant thinker Karl Barth put it, is an open wound in the body of Christ that continually challenges the truth of Christianity. Either Christ is the son of God, as Christianity claims, or he is not, as Judaism claims. Both can't be right, which is why your existence as a Jew will always challenge the Christian's faith. Eliminating this challenge physically, by destroying you as a human being, has not worked. A far more effective alternative is eliminating you as a Jew. This can be and is being done more and more as the barriers between you and the Christian come down.

In fact, there are hardly any of them left. Jews are accepted practically everywhere. You say there are still some country clubs that exclude you? But there are others that exclude Catholics, or even Protestants who aren't wealthy or WASPish enough. To say nothing of blacks. Or Jewish clubs that don't accept non-Jews. The point is that you live in an open and liberal enough society for the temptation to assimilate into it to be very, very great. Or to put it more precisely, for there to be no particularly good reason not to assimilate. The fact is that you're already far along the road to assimilation.

JUDAH: What makes you say that?

ISRAEL: Do you remember what I told you about my stay with my uncle and aunt in Australia? From the minute I arrived in Melbourne there was hardly a day we weren't invited to have dinner with some family. "Everyone wants to meet you," my aunt and uncle said, and it sounded logical enough. In those days before jet travel a young, native-born Israeli was not a common sight Down Under.

It didn't take me long to understand, however, that curiosity and the desire to be nice to a young Israeli were not the only motives. At every dinner I attended there was a young lady in her late teens who was the daughter of my hosts. Today I remember all those girls as a single dark-haired, pale-faced, collective figure that hardly spoke and mostly stared at the table. Which was more than you could say for their parents, especially their mothers. No matter what the conversation was about—life in Israel, the Arabs, the weather—they found a way to work their daughters into it: what good students they were, what good children they were, how interested they were in Israel.

On our way home my aunt would be sure to take up the cudgel.

"Well, what did you think of Sarah? Isn't she sweet?"

"She's all right."

"I think she's absolutely lovely. They say her father has three men's clothing shops and is about to open a fourth in Sydney."

I didn't get it. True, I was tall, young, handsome, and intelligent, and I was sure that if I had had a daughter I would have been happy had she brought me home to meet me with the news that she and I were getting married. But I was also sure, alas, that there were at least twenty thousand other young men in Melbourne who were as good a catch as me. Why all the fuss over me?

In the end it penetrated. There were indeed many other young Melbournians whose credentials were no worse than mine, but most of them had a defect that disqualified them at once: They weren't Jewish. Pity the poor Jewish mother! Here she was with a marriageable son or daughter, and the supply of Jewish mates was much smaller than the demand. And it was a race against time, because every day another name had to be crossed off the scanty list of eligibles. Every day brought closer the horrible possibility that a son or daughter would bring home a shiksa or a goy. What Jewish parents could even think of sleep with such a prospect ahead of them?

And suddenly, like a gift from the blue, there I was. Long before I had arrived in person everyone knew what I looked like, where I had studied, what my marks were, and—most important of all—who my parents were and what they did for a living. It would undoubtedly have helped considerably had my aunt and uncle been richer, but no one said it was easy to be a Jew—and better a Jew with poor relations than a goy or a shiksa with rich ones!

A slab of fresh meat—that's what I was. Not that there wasn't a problem, because if Sarah or Leah actually succeeded in landing me, there was a danger of their ending up in Israel. Only the thought of their marrying a goy was more frightening. How did their mothers cope with such a fear? By using the common sense that every Jewish mother is endowed with. What young man in his right mind would conceivably want to return to Israel when he had a chance to live in Australia and to take over his father-in-law's business there?

And so there was really no reason not to join the stampede, which was ably abetted by my aunt, whose considered opinion it was that "It wouldn't do you any harm to find a nice girl from a good family. I'm sure your mother won't mind if I help you find her."

In the army I had learned how to defend myself, but no defense seemed possible against this onslaught of Jewish mothers. It began the moment they opened their eyes in the morning and ended only when they shut them at night. Before I was out of bed, last night's Jewish mother was already on the phone to find out what I thought of her Leah. Together the two of them, Leah's mother and my aunt, plotted an offense more sophisticated than any battle plan in the world. Frontal attacks were avoided. It was all indirection, feints, insinuation. But day and night. Everywhere. Let the talk be about my studies and my aunt would turn it to Leah's. Let it be about music and I would be told what a wonderful pianist Leah was. Let it be about the movies and lo and behold! there was a wonderful movie playing at the Odeon that Leah was dying to see.

I imagine there are men who could have withstood such assaults. Hercules. Bar-Kochba. Ben-Canaan. Perhaps Rambo. I must confess that I eventually succumbed to my aunt's iron logic, which best expressed itself in the question, "How can you know if you haven't tried?" Twice I asked one of these Jewish maidens out on a date. All I can remember of either occasion is long silences and a desperate search for something to talk about. The poor girls seemed to have been lobotomized by the overwhelming desire to find a proper husband. Even surrounded by an audience in the dark theater, they were accompanied by their mothers. In fact, *they were* their mothers.

Finally, though, I found a lovely girl from a good family. The talk of the world in those days was the capture of Adolf Eichmann. The media were full of how the Nazi butcher had been kidnapped from Argentina and brought to Israel to stand trial for war crimes against the Jewish people. The television channels kept looking for fresh human interest angles—and suddenly they found out that they had a scoop right under their noses: an honest-to-God Israeli newly arrived from the country of Eichmann's accusers. I was interviewed on some program, in the course of which I met its producer, a lovely, intelligent young lady, who, judging from her address, was also from "a good home."

One night I came back from a date with her at three o'clock in the morning. My aunt and uncle were unaccustomedly still awake. They had been waiting for me, they told me. And without further ado they challenged me: "Who's Margaret?"

It seemed that I had been late for our date that night, and that after I had left she had phoned to see where I was. I told them that she was a television producer, very lovely, very intelligent—

"And very goyish!" interrupted my aunt, who had never displayed anger toward me before.

"How do you know?" I asked.

"What do you mean, how do I know? Isn't her name Margaret?"

"Yes, it is."

"Have you ever heard of a Jewish girl named Margaret?"

No, I hadn't. I didn't know a single Jew named Margaret —or, for that matter, Goldie. I was twenty-one years old, and I divided girls into those I liked and those I didn't rather than into Jews and non-Jews. And since I liked Margaret, I didn't give a damn if she was Jewish or not.

My uncle and aunt said that they were responsible for me and had to answer to my mother. Therefore, they added, issuing an ultimatum, I had to stop seeing Margaret. And when I told them that I had no intention of doing so, my aunt declared in a frail, tear-choked voice that in that case I could no longer live with them.

I moved out and found a place of my own. I wasn't angry. They were good people. The best I had ever met. I knew it took years off their lives to throw me out of their home. I knew that my relationship with a shiksa—what their friends and neighbors would say, the shame they would have to bear—was more than they could live with.

JUDAH: Times have changed.

ISRAEL: I know. And that's the point. It's nothing to be upset about or ashamed of anymore.

Not long ago I visited a small city in the Middle West. At one of the functions I attended I was seated next to an intelligent career woman in her forties. Between the salad and the eternal chicken she told me about her children, a twenty-four-year-old son and a nineteen-year-old daughter. Her son had been a good student, was doing well at work, and had a girlfriend he had been living with for two years. "That's wonderful," I said automatically. "What more could you ask for?" "Only that the girlfriend should be Jewish," she replied with a note of sadness. But she soon got over it. "As long as she's a good person and they're happy," she said. The same went for her daughter, who, it turned out, also had a non-Jewish boyfriend.

That was news to me. Big news. Fifteen or twenty years ago the same woman would have viewed it as a tragedy. She would have been ashamed of it. She certainly would never had mentioned it to a stranger. And she wouldn't have forgiven her children for it either. Better for them to be unhappy with a Jew than happy with a non-Jew. Not that she would have put it that way. She would have dismissed the question by telling herself that her children could not possibly be happy with a non-Jewish partner, since the difference between "us" and "them" was too great. Twenty or thirty years ago, perhaps even less, you yourself would have considered your child's marrying out a personal and social tragedy. What would the neighbors say? What would your fellow synagogue members say? Nothing that you would want to hear. They might nod in sympathy, but in the privacy of their own homes they would remark, "That's what happens when you don't bring up your children right."

Today you accept it. That's obvious from how you talk about it, from how you think about it—and from the statistics. In the 1940s only 7 percent of you intermarried.

In the early sixties it was 17 percent. Now it's close to half, and according to some figures, even higher.

This is not an unknown phenomenon in the third generation of an immigrant population. It's also no doubt a function of the enormous increase in permissiveness that has taken place in American society in recent decades. One way or another, however, today it's no longer tragic. It's acceptable.

Shall I tell you something? It's even more than that. Lately I've begun to notice that you're actually happy about it. The proof is that once, if your child wanted to marry a non-Jew, you insisted that the latter at least convert. Today it hardly matters anymore.

JUDAH: Maybe because in the meantime I've discovered—

ISRAEL: Don't tell me! Do me a favor and don't say it . . .

JUDAH: But you don't even know what I want to say!

ISRAEL: You want to say that you've discovered that it results in more Jews.

JUDAH: But it does! Many non-Jews who are married to Jews begin to take an interest in Judaism. Many children of mixed couples receive a Jewish education. The studies show that we gain more Jews than we lose by it.

ISRAEL: In that case it should be encouraged.

JUDAH: What should be?

ISRAEL: Intermarriage. Your slogan should be, "Help the Jews by marrying out!"

JUDAH: I never said that.

ISRAEL: But why shouldn't you say it? According to you, intermarriage will not only increase the Jewish population, it will eventually wipe out Christianity!

JUDAH: You're going to an absurd extreme.

ISRAEL: That's America. You can always find some expert there to conduct a study whose results will be just what you're looking for. Today all the scientific evidence is that oatmeal reduces cholesterol—tomorrow it will be that it does everything except reduce cholesterol. If I read about a study proving that decaf doesn't raise your blood pressure, I know that another study showing that it does isn't far behind.

The fact is that every serious study has proven what hardly needs proof—that is, that intermarriage reduces the number of Jews. It's a process that begins with the first generation to marry out and accelerates with the second. Only about a quarter of the children of intermarried parents identify as Jews when they grow up. How could it be otherwise? But it was inevitable that you would commission some study proving the unprovable. After all, you live in the land not only of unlimited opportunity, but also of unlimited opportunism.

The most crucial and interesting development is that in most intermarriages, over 60 percent of them, the non-Jewish partner does not convert. You no longer insist on it. In fact, you don't even bother to request it. After all, you're a liberal and pro-freedom of choice, aren't you? But that's not the real reason. Certainly, it's not the main one. Intellectual arguments in themselves never move you. They always go hand in hand with more practical considerations. If you don't like having to walk to synagogue on Saturday, you invent a new form of Judaism that allows you to drive in the name of freedom of religion. If you would rather Jews from the Soviet Union immigrated to

121

America and not to Israel, you become a passionate supporter of freedom of choice.

The real reason is that you've come to the conclusion that it's pointless to ask the non-Jewish partner to convert. What for? If your children and grandchildren continue living in America, why is it so important for them to remain Jewish? So that they can go on asking themselves all their lives who they are and why? So that they should never stop hearing snide remarks about their Jewishness? So that they should always feel outsiders, no matter where they live? So that the threat of an anti-Semitic outburst should always hang over them? So that they should be badgered incessantly with the problems of Israel as a means of extorting money for a country with which they identify less and less? So that they should have to attend Temple on Friday night instead of watching TV or going out? So that their children should grow up as you did with the embarrassing memory of getting on the Sunday School bus, ashamed of the stares of their non-Jewish friends?

What for? Isn't it better to belong to the majority? Isn't it better to live a normal life and not be an abnormal minority?

JUDAH: You haven't heard me complaining, have you? Living as a minority doesn't bother me.

ISRAEL: So you say—but the rate at which you're assimilating and the toleration you show for it say the opposite. Please don't get me wrong. I have nothing against all that. If I lived in America and considered it my home, I would want my children to cross the lines, too. Not with half a foot, not with one foot, but with both feet bearing body and soul firmly on the ground. I'd encourage them to marry non-Jews and bring up their children as perfect Gentiles.

JUDAH: Why?

ISRAEL: Why not?

JUDAH: Because they're Jews!

ISRAEL: I'd much rather my children be happy than Jewish. I can't think of a better application of the saying, "If you can't beat them, join them." After all, we only live once, so why not get the most out of it, short and problematical as it is? When I see how you live with your agreed-on lies and compromises, I know I wouldn't want my children to be like you. That's why I would want them to belong to the majority.

JUDAH: Don't you take any pride in your heritage?

ISRAEL: You see? That's another good reason for not wanting my children to be like you. What did you actually say now? Nothing. You simply used an empty phrase that you've adopted without even bothering to think about what it means.

What kind of pride in your heritage are you talking about? At a reception in Toronto several years ago I was approached by one of the wealthiest members of the Jewish community (he had made his money, lots of it, in real estate), who presented me with his visiting card at once: "I'm proud to be a Jew." In vain I tried hushing the devil's advocate inside me. "Why?" I asked. The man was flabbergasted. He had never asked himself that question and certainly did not expect to be asked it by a Jew from Israel. Ever since he would remember he had been told by his parents and teachers and friends that he should be proud to be a Jew, and never once had it occurred to him that this called for an explanation. "What do you mean, why?" he stammered. "There's our . . . our . . . heritage, there's the . . . the Bible . . ."

"Did you create that heritage?" I asked. "Did you write the Bible?"

"But . . . but I'm . . . I'm part of it all . . ."

"Only by accident," I answered him. "By total accident. Because you were born a Jew. If you had been born a Protestant you would be proud of the heritage of Martin Luther, and if you had been born a Muslim, of the heritage of Muhammed. Tell me something: If you had been born a Catholic or a Buddhist, would you convert to be part of the Jewish heritage you're so proud of? Of course not. You would be proud of being a Christian or a Buddhist. If you're Jewish anyway, I can understand wanting to feel good about it for the same price. But why make a big deal of it?

JUDAH: But what about the Jewish genius?

ISRAEL: What does the genius of an Einstein have to do with you or me? I might understand it if Albert's mother or father were proud of him—but what does that have to do with either of us?

I ask you, then: What's so worthwhile and important about being a Jew? Being different? Being kept out of the country club? Being led to the gas chambers? If you're living in America anyway, wouldn't it be better to be a Christian, and better yet, Protestant?

JUDAH: Intermarriage is a danger in Israel, too.

ISRAEL: Intermarriage between whom?

JUDAH: Between Jews and Arabs.

ISRAEL: You might as well say that intermarriage in America is a danger to Christians. Intermarriage endangers the minority, not the majority. I have enough problems without you saddling me with another that doesn't in fact exist. If you were to admit that intermarriage jeopardizes your existence as a Jew, you might be forced to conclude that ensuring your future meant coming to live with me. And since that's the one thing you don't want to do, you have to convince yourself that the same dangers or worse ones exist with the alternative.

That's one reason you keep avoiding the issue of intermarriage. Another is that you'll keep away from it anyway if you know what's good for you. After all, a growing number of your own leaders—UJA chairmen, heads of bonds drives, presidents of other Jewish organizations—are intermarried themselves. Not that they need to tell you to lay off the subject. You're smart enough to do it without being told if you want to keep your place in the community.

One Jew who didn't understand this reality was a certain rabbi at Washington's Temple Sinai. In one of his sermons he pointed out—very, very cautiously—that, Jewishly speaking, intermarriage is not such a good idea. That was all. He didn't say that it was impermissible or harmful or the direct route to Jewish extinction, and he made sure not to sound the least note of personal criticism. Nevertheless, the temple board met and decided to fire him, relenting only when the poor spiritual leader promised never to raise the issue again.

Of course, I'm aware that despite the dramatic changes in your attitude, you're still uncomfortable with marrying non-Jews. Like the Jewish woman from Chicago who happened to be exceptionally tall. She had a hard time finding a potential husband her size until finally she did come across one. The only drawback was that he wasn't Jewish. She agreed to marry him on one condition. No, it wasn't that he should convert. And it wasn't that they raise their children as Jews, either. It was that they live in a Jewish neighborhood. When her friends asked her why she insisted on it, she answered with a perfectly straight face: "Because I hate goyim."

But I'm sure you'll get over that.

PUTTING ONE OVER ON GOD

JUDAH: I don't get you. You talk and act like a total secularist, in fact, like an atheist. And yet on the other hand you let a small Orthodox minority control many aspects of your life and pass laws forbidding you to worship God in a non-Orthodox fashion—in a Reform one, for example, to mention the denomination to which the largest group of American Jews belongs.

ISRAEL: Welcome back to the vicious circle! It's like this: I live in a democratic country that has elections. The result of these elections leaves each of the two major parties short of a majority in the Knesset and in need of the small religious parties in order to form a government. The religious parties can write their terms because they are able to tip the balance either way. That's the political reality. I don't like it, but I can't change it. Only you can.

JUDAH: Me? How?

ISRAEL: By being here. You could help create a new political map on which the religious parties would lose their power. It's the same story all over again: You claim that you can't live in Israel because of the strength of the Orthodox, but this strength exists because you don't come to live here. In true vicious-circle fashion, you keep trying to get the best of both worlds by blaming me for your own failure. Or to put it differently: By not living in Israel you create the reality that excuses your not living in Israel.

JUDAH: Try and see this from my point of view. I'm not an atheist Sabra. I'm not an ultra-Orthodox Jew. I'm Reform or Conservative. With the laws of your state and your way of thinking that reject any form of Judaism that is not Orthodox, there is no room for my brand of religion.

ISRAEL: That's because your Reform and Conservative formulas have no relevance in Israel. As an Israeli, I'm not even sure that I know what these movements are. That is, I know what they stand for, but I fail to understand the justification for their existence. Simple Jew that I am, I know what traditional Jewish practice is, and so it seems to me that if you're a believing Jew, you're also a practicing Jew, and that if you're a practicing Jew, you worship God as Judaism has worshiped Him over the centuries.

JUDAH: How typical that is of you Israelis. Stubborn, extreme in your position, not ready, maybe not even able, to understand other views, to be tolerant of any life-style that differs from yours. I find it impossible to believe that you prefer the obscure and backward extremism of Orthodoxy to the progressivism of Conservatism and Reform.

ISRAEL: What we prefer is the real thing to the imitation, honesty to hypocrisy. Just as I respect God too much to believe in Him, so I respect Judaism too much to accept a diluted alternative.

JUDAH: You have a right to your own views and beliefs and we to ours, isn't that right? Or do you insist that we should be like you or not exist at all? We believe in certain forms of religion that you reject. That's your privilege. But what about ours? Don't you recognize my right to worship God in whatever way I choose?

ISRAEL: Of course I do. As far as I'm concerned, you can worship Him while standing on your head. I intellectually respect that right, too, as long as it's based on genuine religious beliefs and emotions, just as I equally respect anyone who honestly feels that the language or form of the prayerbook does not reflect his sense of God, or that he does not need formal holidays and services to express his religious devotion and love.

The key word is "honestly." What you do, however, strikes me as typical of the way you do everything: You fabricate a belief to suit your convenience. Orthodox worship in America is inconvenient. For one thing, you don't want to have to walk to services, especially once you have moved to the suburbs. In the old urban Jewish neighborhoods there was always a synagogue within walking distance, but once you had money you wanted a big suburban house. Well, why not? It's just that the people in such houses live far apart, and walking to synagogue, especially in cold winter weather, is far from pleasant. And so you made yourself a religion that allowed you to drive your big car right up to the entrance of the synagogue. If I know America, the day isn't far when you'll have drive-in synagogues that won't make you leave your car at all.

JUDAH: I'm sorry to inform you that Reform Judaism already existed in the nineteenth century when automobiles had not been invented.

ISRAEL: You're speaking of German Reform. It's true that the Reform movement in America came from a German Jewish background. But if you look into the history of the Reform movement in Germany, you'll see that there, too, its ideology of modernism was little more than a pretext for desires very much like yours.

In any event, the Reform movement in America was in its infancy then. It began to gain ground early in this century, with the second generation of Jewish immigrants from Eastern Europe. The first generation was still Orthodox. Their children, who were economically better off, switched to Reform.

JUDAH: Or to Conservatism.

ISRAEL: Which is a compromise between Reform and Orthodoxy, a halfway house for those who find the direct route to Reform too quick.

JUDAH: You're overlooking the fact that I could have chosen to attend no synagogue at all.

ISRAEL: No, you couldn't have. Because the synagogue, or the temple as you prefer to call it, is not just a place for religious worship, it's the center of your communal life. It's where you have your get-togethers, it's where you get married, it's where your son is bar-mitzvahed. Not attend-

ing it means cutting your ties with the Jewish community—
and that's something you can't afford to do, both for social
and economic reasons.

Besides which, you *do* want a bit of Jewishness in your
life. You're not willing to do without it altogether, although
more and more you have less and less of it. You just don't
want that Jewishness to come in too large doses or in ways
that might prove inconvenient. Like having to walk to
synagogue. Or like having to keep kosher. After all, you
find yourself dining more and more with non-Jews and
shrimp is undeniably delectable, while pork no longer
gives you a stomach ache either. But being a conventional
fellow, you're not about to say, not even to yourself, "To
hell with all the laws and rituals, I feel like crab salad and
crab salad is what I'm having." That would make you a
rebel, which is not something worth being in your society.
And so you've come up with a religious movement that
allows you to believe that you're okay without having to
give up your comforts and—perhaps most important of
all—your desire to be like the Gentiles. Orthodoxy was all
very well as long as you were not so wealthy and were
confined to your own small Jewish neighborhoods. The
more money you had, the more involved with non-Jews
you became, Orthodox worship and customs began to
embarrass you, because they no longer corresponded to
your new status. No problem, though: You live in America,
where everything is a question of supply and demand. If
there's a demand for a new religious movement, the supply
won't lag far behind. And indeed, now you have a Jewish
denomination that doesn't allow even the Gentiles to
define you as different. You've traded the skullcap for lots

of pomp, a rabbi who resembles a successful businessman, and of course, an organ.

What you've done is what Professor Yeshayahu Leibowitz has called, "Renouncing the commandments of the Torah in the name of Judaism." According to Leibowitz, that is the great sin of Christianity. In the hands of Jews it becomes even greater.

JUDAH: Leibowitz is an observant Jew himself, and it's possible to understand his point of view and his discomfort. But you? Perhaps I'm mistaken, but I thought you weren't religious . . .

ISRAEL: You thought right. But you annoy me anyway, because you're trying to put one over on God by taking His religion and tradition and rearranging it to suit your own needs. At your Passover seder you tell your children that the exodus from Egypt was simply a struggle against slavery and turn Moses into Abraham Lincoln. After all, the Exodus was meant not only to free them from slavery but to enable them to establish a home of their own in the Promised Land. Presenting it as such is awkward for you, however, because it sounds too much like aliyah. And so you give it a little face-lift and turn a struggle for national liberation into an abolitionist campaign.

On Hanukkah you go it one better. Standing with your children by the burning candles, you tell them that the war of the Maccabees against the Greeks was a battle for . . . religious freedom. "Now, dear boys and girls," runs the implicit message, "do you understand what the Maccabees were fighting for? For the establishment of Reform Judaism in America!" The fact is, of course, that the Maccabees were fighting for the right to worship God in one way alone, which was the only way they knew. Had other Jews tried worshiping Him differently, the Maccabees would have fought them no less than the Greeks—as their descendants indeed fought the followers of Jesus two centuries later.

JUDAH: I still don't understand. If you're not religious yourself, what difference does any of this make to you?

ISRAEL: That's a good question. Maybe it's because it seems undignified to me. Maybe it's because of the intellectual hypocrisy you wrap it in. Maybe if you just came out and said that you prefer Reform Judaism because it let you do what you want, I wouldn't mind it so much.

JUDAH: And Orthodoxy doesn't have its own legalistic ways of fooling God, too, like asking Gentiles to do forbidden work on the Sabbath or pretending to sell them a Jew's leavened food on Passover?

ISRAEL: I hope you don't intend to make me a spokesman for Orthodoxy. Of course it has its share of hypocrisy, just like all religions do. Still, it's a single, unified movement with authoritative forums to decide what is right and what is wrong. There's something phony about a religion in which you start a new movement whenever something doesn't please you. Besides, isn't the hypocrisy of Orthodoxy enough for you without your having to add to it?

JUDAH: Do you believe in God?

ISRAEL: No.

JUDAH: Then why on earth should you care if I put one over on Him?

ISRAEL: Because I respect Him.

JUDAH: But you don't believe He exists!

ISRAEL: Because I respect Him. That's why I rule out His existence. My respect for the Divinity is so great that I give it the benefit of the doubt. Because if I believed in its existence, I would have to stop respecting it.

JUDAH: How's that?

ISRAEL: How could I respect a Being that's responsible for the world we live in: death at an early age, children dying of hunger, millions of innocent people butchered yearly? If there is a God, then He's responsible for all these atrocities, and if He's responsible, He's a monster. I don't want to believe in the monstrosity of the Divinity. That's why I prefer believing in its nonexistence.

JUDAH: But we're talking about a Being whose acts and motives neither you nor I can comprehend. That's what makes it Divine.

ISRAEL: I'm afraid that argument is beyond me. I envy those who can honestly accept it. Life is easier for them. I suppose I simply lack the imagination to conceive of a reason why children should starve to death or people should be massacred. It's more than I'm capable of. I can't understand why the world couldn't have been created without cholesterol. And if there had to be cholesterol, why chocolate? Only a malicious power could invent such a catch. And since I don't want to believe that God is evil, I give Him the credit of not being at all.

For this same reason, however, I expect those who do believe in Him and in the purity of His motives to show Him no less respect. That's why it offends me to see someone try to put one over on Him. And that's what you Reform Jews do all the time.

JUDAH: Nevertheless, as flawed as Reform Judaism may be, I would rather have a Jew who prays in a Reform temple than a Jew who doesn't pray at all. I think that of the two, the templegoer stands a better chance of remaining Jewish.

ISRAEL: I'm sorry I can't agree with you. Because you're not only putting one over on God, you're unwittingly putting one over on yourselves. You've made Judaism so much like Christianity that little by little, with the help of intermarriage, you're turning into a Christian. If Conservatism is the first step away from Judaism, Reform is the first step toward Christianity. It's a fact that most Jews who intermarry come from Reform families, followed by Conservatives. There's almost no intermarriage among the Orthodox.

JUDAH: It would seem to me a reasonable assumption, however, that without Reform you would lose more Jews sooner.

ISRAEL: Why? A secularist can be just as respectful of religious tradition, provided there's something to respect. By its very nature Reform is a prostitution of religion. That's why there's no use you can't put it to. It's amazing how many Jewish youngsters suddenly discovered they wanted to be Reform rabbis at the time of the Vietnam War, when divinity school kept you out of the army, just as it's amazing how quickly the same youngsters lost all interest in the rabbinate as soon as the war was over.

Once you begin to play fast and loose with religion,

anything goes. Like the rabbi in the small Middle Western community who had a problem: He needed an assistant and couldn't find anyone to come to such an out-of-the-way place. So what did he do? He hired a local Protestant to help him worship the Jewish God. The board of the synagogue decided he had gone too far and forced him to dismiss his new employee, but he himself saw nothing wrong with it. I sympathize with him. He may not have been conscious of what he was doing, but by doing it he was declaring that the emperor was naked. Reform Judaism is not a religious movement. Reform Judaism is a contrivance to enable non-believing Jews to think that they believe. And if a contrivance is all that it is, why shouldn't the assistant rabbi be a Protestant? I'm certain that one of these days, when the labor shortage grows greater, Reform synagogues will let their rabbis hire Gentiles. If Reform is a first step toward Christianity anyway, what could be more logical?

Something tells me, though, that I'm not telling you anything new. I think you know all this already. I think that deep down you too realize that there is something very un-Jewish in Reform. That's why you go on supporting Orthodoxy even while intellectually opposing it. Take, for instance, the Lubavitcher Hasidim, one of Orthodoxy's bastions in America, who hold a gala fund-raising dinner every year in Los Angeles that is attended by your best and your brightest—Jewish movie moguls, artists, and film stars, all of the Reform persuasion.

Why? What makes you support the Lubavitcher *rebbe* when he looks upon you with revulsion? The reason is that in the privacy of your thoughts you know that his followers and their ilk are the real, the authentic Jews and that Orthodoxy alone can preserve Judaism in time of trouble. Not Reform. Not Conservatism. Orthodoxy.

JUDAH: You don't know what you're talking about. These Jews disgust me. With their gloomy black clothes and their arrogance, their ridiculous sidelocks, the smell of sweat they give off, their isolation, their occupations as diamond merchants and usurers. They repel me and embarrass me because by their appearance and behavior they give Judaism a bad name.

ISRAEL: What's that got to do with it? I don't like them much more than you do. But let's be honest. If a new Inquisition were to start up today and we were all led to the torture chambers, which of us would refuse to give up his Judaism, even in the face of death? You and I know very well that when it came to the supreme test, it would only be these ridiculous, annoying, smelly people. Not you or I. That's why, although you are ashamed of these ultra-Orthodox Jews, although you shun their company, although you despise them, although you didn't come to their defense in the summer of 1991, when the enraged black residents of Crown Heights carried out a pogrom against them, despite all that, you still know they are the keepers of the Jewish faith. Therefore you want them to continue in their clannish and peculiar ways. What you *don't* want is for their continued existence to require any personal sacrifice on your part, and that's why you have created your own modern forms of religion.

My whole point is that I don't need such a framework, or any religious framework at all, to maintain my Jewishness. And neither, if you were to live here, would you. In Israel there's no need for a temple to feel Jewishness—the streets are full of it. Yom Kippur in Israel is something you notice whether you want to or not, and there's no need to drive to synagogue, because there are synagogues all around you. I don't need religion to feel my Jewish identity here. That's why Reform Judaism is irrelevant to Israeli life and its second-rate status in Israel is no reason for you not to be part of that life.

JUDAH: Meanwhile, there's constant discussion in Israel of a new "Who Is A Jew?" law that will not recognize Reform conversion. Its passage would be a slap in the face to us.

ISRAEL: It hasn't been passed yet. But suppose it is. Why should it bother you?

JUDAH: Because many Americans born to Reform-converted mothers will not be recognized by you as Jews.

ISRAEL: Ordinary American Jews aren't lining up to live in Israel, and you're trying to tell me that such Jews will?

JUDAH: Not today, but . . .

ISRAEL: Don't you see what you're asking from me? You want me to live according to your needs, not because if I do you'll join me, but because some day, perhaps, if you're driven out of America (and then, too, you'll most likely go elsewhere), you just may possibly end up living in Israel at some indefinite date in the future!

I suggest, then, that we drop the subject. If you come to live in Israel, I promise to show you how to remain Jewish without Reform Judaism. And if that's not enough for you, you have recourse to standard democratic practice: Win over a majority of the voting populace and pass whatever laws you wish. If you succeed, you can even make Reform the state religion of Israel. What could be fairer and more reasonable?

So tell me: Are you coming?

JUDAH: Just a minute. There are other reasons why I'm not.

ISRAEL: I thought so. All right, let's take a look at them.

THE BURDEN OF SMALLNESS

JUDAH: You say that you want me to emigrate to Israel. But just look at your economic situation. You can barely support the population you have now.

ISRAEL: My problem is not the economy. My main problem is survival. Nearly every day I am reminded of a story about Henry Kissinger, who was your secretary of state during the Nixon and Ford administrations.

In 1974, after the Yom Kippur War, Kissinger ran shuttle negotiations between Jerusalem and Damascus in order to achieve a disengagement of forces. Toward the end of his travels he had a conversation with Syrian president Hafez al-Assad that took a philosophical turn. Kissinger had asked Assad to make concessions on the Golan Heights. "Give me one good reason why I should," Assad said.

"To make possible an agreement," answered Kissinger.

"But why should I want an agreement," Assad asked, "when all we Arabs have to do is wait patiently for Israel to disappear of its own accord? The Jews of the world

138

don't want to live in it and the world itself will grow tired of it. Why reach agreements with it? Just in order to help it survive?"

That's the main problem. You take my existence for granted, although it is far from a certainty. Actually, in the domain of economics, I don't think I'm doing badly. Even though I spend proportionally more on defense than any other country in the world, have no natural resources to speak of, and am a small country living with the constant threat of annihilation, no one is dying of hunger in my streets and everyone has full medical coverage.

Still, though I don't ask to be pitied, I do want you to know that I pay much more for a standard of living that, in both individual and national terms, is considerably lower than yours. There are several reasons for this, the main one being my small scale. It's hard to maintain a robust economy with such a small population. Which brings me back to you once more. Can you imagine what we might accomplish with, say, another 2 million educated, technologically sophisticated Jews who are the products of an advanced industrial society? Do you have any idea of what they could do for us economically? To begin with, the local market would increase dramatically. Secondly, my economy would become far more efficient and productive, which would give a big boost to exports. You would bring with you one of the things I need most, namely, a talent for entrepreneurship that is not dependent on bureaucrats and government functionaries. You would bring with you all the ingredients of your success in America. You would bring yourself—both as a producer and a consumer.

Instead of all that, though, what do we actually have? The vicious circle again. You say you can't come because of the economic situation in Israel when the economic situation in Israel is a corollary of your not coming.

JUDAH: Suppose I did come. Could you absorb so many people? I see what difficulties you have in absorbing immigration from the Soviet Union.

ISRAEL: That's just another vicious-circle argument, because if you came the entire situation would be different. The immigrants from the Soviet Union are coming without a cent, from an economically and productively backward society. They need to be supplied with all their needs and taught things that I, let alone you, take for granted.

So, of course, such an immigration is difficult for me to absorb. But you're another kettle of fish entirely. Your coming would improve my situation to the point where I—we—could absorb Soviet Jews and their hardships far more easily.

JUDAH: You're not being realistic. Where will you house me? Where will you find work for me? You're talking big numbers.

ISRAEL: Yes, but America isn't Russia or Morocco. You're not fleeing a chaotic society. If I knew you were coming, I could prepare for you in an orderly fashion. I've been waiting for you for forty years—I wouldn't have to bring you all at once now. I could spread it over a reasonable period.

I also don't think you would need that much help from me. You have the money, you have the know-how, you have the efficiency. If you decided that that's what you wanted to do, I'm sure you'd have no trouble doing it. Since you don't want to do it, though, you take refuge in the vicious circle. You tell me that I'm too small and weak to absorb you. But why am I small and weak? Because you haven't come. First you make me small and weak by not coming, and then you use it as an excuse not to come!

JUDAH: Do you want to know something? Perhaps I might come to live in Israel, but I have children who would have to go to the army there. I could never forgive myself if something happened to them.

ISRAEL: Do *you* want to know something? Of all the reasons you've given me, that's the most insulting and offensive. You won't forgive yourself if anything should happen to one of your children—but you'll forgive yourself easily enough if anything should happen to one of mine. And it's more likely to happen to a child of mine if you don't come.

Because the tragic vicious circle is at work here, too. Give me 2 million modern, well-trained, efficient Jews and most of my security problems will be solved.

JUDAH: How? Will my coming make the Arabs hate you less?

ISRAEL: There are about 4 million Jews in Israel today. Should the rosiest predictions of immigration from Russia come true, Israel would still be a country inhabited by a tiny populace divided against itself in all kinds of ways: by religion, by culture, by politics, by education, by mentality. The result is a demoralized society that is socially and economically weak. There is nothing unrealistic about

141

hoping that such a society will not last. The thought of destroying it need not be merely a dream.

JUDAH: Oh, come one. The past proves that you know how to look after yourself very well. You've come out of every war on top.

ISRAEL: Is that so? What past? Which war? I came out of the Yom Kippur War by the skin of my teeth. In fact, in that war I was on the verge of defeat and only the gross errors of the Arabs—and the American assistance that came very late—then saved me from destruction. Or maybe you are referring to the Lebanon War—that horrible mistake which spilled my blood without attaining even the limited goal of throwing the terrorists out of Lebanon.

You don't understand—maybe you don't want to understand—that the reassuring story of the clever, agile, and resourceful Israeli David confronting the stupid and clumsy Arab Goliath is over and done with. David has put on a lot of weight in the meantime, he thinks about himself more than his country, and his motivation to protect that country is greatly diminished. Goliath, on the other hand, has become far more sophisticated, more daring, better equipped, and much more strongly motivated. For all these reasons, there won't be another marvelous victory like the Six Day War. Now it's long-range missiles, chemical warheads, maybe even nuclear weapons. So I suggest that you open your eyes, see reality as it is, recognize the fact that our existence in Israel is placed in question every day and every hour. And acknowledge that we certainly will *not* be able to ensure this precarious existence in our present situation.

On the other hand, a country of 6 or 7 million Jews in which, culturally and economically, the human factor would lean more to the plus side, would be practically indestructible. And since a war with such a country would then become a fruitless effort to attain the unattainable, the motivation for making peace would be much greater.

JUDAH: It takes two to tango, and meanwhile you don't seem to me at all ready to decide whether you are willing to make compromises for peace.

ISRAEL: Because of you, damn it all! What do I have now? Not enough people and too many problems. No end of anxieties. An incessant preoccupation with survival. If, say, 2 million of you were to come, it would be a totally different story. I would be much bigger. Much stronger. I could make more concessions and take greater risks. The question of territorial concessions is not just a human and political one, it's above all a question of demography. Many Israelis support territorial concessions because they know that, given the difference between Arab and Jewish birth rates, we might think otherwise if enough of you came to change the demographic balance.

JUDAH: Then the key to an Arab-Israeli peace settlement is in my hands. Is that what you're trying to say?

ISRAEL: Does that sound so outrageous to you?

JUDAH: I certainly don't share your confidence that 2 million American Jews would make that much difference.

ISRAEL: I can't guarantee you that they would. But you must agree it's not illogical. And you certainly should be honest enough to admit that it would guarantee a fairer sharing of the burden between us. The more Jews there are in Israel, the less taxes each of us will have to pay. We'll have more working hands and more purchasing power. We'll have more soldiers, so that my son's regular army service can be cut from three years to two or even one. Less of our youngsters might leave the country. More of yours might come. The burden might become a little lighter . . .

If it weren't for the vicious circle.

4

❧

The Conspiracy of Silence
and Deceit

A HUMAN DUMPING GROUNDS

JUDAH: You talk about me as though I were a monolith, which isn't at all the case. I'm composed of Jews who don't care about Israel and of Jews who care about it greatly. Some of my organizations are Zionist and some aren't. There's a difference.

ISRAEL: I know you're not a monolith. But there's one thing you're extremely monolithic about, and that's aliyah. You can call yourself a Zionist or a non-Zionist or a neo-Zionist, you can be a liberal or a conservative, you can be rich or poor—when it comes to the question of living in Israel, there is perfect unanimity among you.

Allow me to make a comparison. We in Israel are aware that in our conflict with the Arabs we have doves and hawks, right-wingers and left-wingers, territorial maximalists and territorial minimalists. That's true enough, but it has relevance only for us, within the context of our own internal quarrels. From an Arab point of view it's absolutely irrelevant. All the Arabs see are Israelis who won't return what, in their view, belongs to them. Whether they won't return more or won't return less is an unimportant distinction for them.

It's the same thing here. What does it matter to me that a Jew cares greatly about Israel if the upshot is that he acts or doesn't act exactly like the Jew who doesn't care at all?

What is the difference between the leaders of your so-called Zionist organizations and the leaders of your non-Zionist ones, like the American Jewish Congress and B'nai B'rith? The former don't want to hear about aliyah and neither do the latter. What is the difference between

147

the conservative rabbi who declares that Israel is beside the point because America is the Promised Land and the president of the Zionist organization who preaches the centrality of Israel to Jewish life but does everything to discourage his son from settling there? Do you know what a supposed Zionist like that does if his son dares utter the "A-word"? He goes to the aliyah desk of the Jewish Agency and scolds: "Isn't it enough that I give Israel money every year without your taking my son from me? Why don't you go pick on the child of a noncontributor!" And if nevertheless the young man insists, his father says, "All right, but first finish college," or "Fine, but only after you've gotten a few years of work experience under your belt," knowing full well that in the meantime the boy will marry, have a child or two, and be too involved in his business to think about such foolishness anymore.

So what good does it do me to be loved by such a man? What's in it for me if he announces fervently at every rally that "Israel will live forever?"

On the contrary: I prefer the declared non-Zionists who say openly that Israel is unimportant for them and that living in it is the last thing on their minds. At least they're telling me the truth, which is more than can be said for your professional breast-beaters who cry on my shoulders how hard it is for them to have to stay in America. Yes, nothing would make them happier than living in Israel— it's just that . . .

Take the professor from Canada whom I've known for the past twenty years. Whenever I run into him—there's not a major Jewish convention that he doesn't attend—he tells me lachrymosely that he may be physically in Canada but his heart is in Israel. Perhaps next year. He thinks so much about living in Israel that he can't even sleep at night. Not to worry, though. His insomnia still hasn't killed him. In fact, he looks remarkably healthy. He's made a fine career in the Jewish world out of his soul-searching. I daresay that if you can do that elegantly enough, you can get to the top of Jewish America even without a lot of money.

Incidentally, I can't deny that this professor has shown his love for Israel in at least one way: He's married to an Israeli woman. Which means that not only hasn't he given Israel one more Jew, he's taken one away. There's true Israel-love for you!

I'll tell you something else, too: not only do I prefer the non-Zionists who lay it on the line, I think that their opposites who pretend to love me are far more dangerous to me. With the first group I at least know where I stand. They make no bones about my not being able to count on them. You, on the other hand, send me messages that might delude me into thinking you're reliable when in fact you're no more reliable than they are.

JUDAH: You really can't see the difference between a Jew who wants to help Israel and a Jew who doesn't? Between a Jew who visits it and a Jew who does not? Between a Jew who cares about it and a Jew for whom it might as well be Nigeria? A Jew like me at least has a commitment to you. That commitment may some day dwindle, as you say, but at present it exists. Isn't that worth something—more, in any case, than no commitment at all?

ISRAEL: No, it isn't, because it merely serves as a distraction. The commitment you have today, which consists of money and lip service, permits both of us to sweep the real problem under the rug. If we could get rid of both the money and the lip service and confront each other without the intellectual rationalizations that distort our relationship, we would have to ask each other, where do we go from here? What do we do to save us both from extinction?

But instead of that you cloak me with your caring, and I, poor affection-starved incompetent that I am, let myself be warmed by it when I should be calling for sincerity and not warmth.

JUDAH: What do you mean by sincerity?

ISRAEL: I'll give you an example. On the record, you're not against aliyah. Your official policy is that it's a good thing. Not good for you personally, not good for your own children, but unobjectionable as a matter of abstract principle.

In other words, you'll never say in plain words that you're against it, even though everything you do says just that.

Let me tell you about two events I witnessed in Toronto.

The first was a "Negev Dinner" in honor of one of the wealthiest Jews in town, the owner of a large men's clothing-store chain. He himself was not a particularly big donor, but the money machine thought it could use him to obtain donations from others. The dinner was held at one of Toronto's fanciest hotels. All the leaders of the Jewish community, which is to say, all its rich men, turned out for the occasion. Black-tie, elegant evening dresses, diamonds, sweet scents of the most expensive perfume, a lavish meal, and an Israeli minister for a speaker flown in specially from Tel Aviv.

The next day there was a farewell party for a family leaving to settle in Israel. The scene: a small, stuffy basement auditorium in the synagogue of a far-out suburb. The cast: a few friends and family members, and not a single prominent member of the community. Ordinary trousers, shirts, sweaters, simple dresses, costume jewelry, a damp smell of mildew, cold chicken with stringbeans. And, of course, no speaker from Israel.

The feeling I was left with was that not only is aliyah something you're not wild about, it's something that frightens you, because, God forbid, it might be catching. It has to be quarantined like a contagious disease. Somehow you considered the family in question to have taken leave of its senses. No one in his right mind would get up and leave Toronto for Israel. Unless, that is, he was retirement age, had a handsome income, and could buy himself a condo in Jerusalem with a view of the Old City and a plot for himself and his wife on the Mount of Olives—without having to give up his other homes in Toronto and Miami Beach, of course. A few months here, a few months there. That kind of living in Israel is acceptable, even fashionable.

JUDAH: What's wrong with it?

ISRAEL: Wrong? Nothing's wrong with it, expect that if you ask me, I'd rather such a Jew stayed home. Ben-Gurion already said in his day that we need live Jews in Israel, not dead ones. But with you it's just the opposite. To come to Israel to live is madness. To be sent there in a coffin, that's okay.

151

JUDAH: You simply don't understand. For the Jews who ask to be buried in Israel it's like going home. Like Joseph whose bones were carried out of Egypt to be buried in the promised land.

ISRAEL: That promise won't exist for long if you go on sending us dead bodies instead of live people. Neither one of us will have a promised land if you continue to promote the attitude that anyone coming to live here is deranged. That it's only for weirdos and others who can't hack it. No normal, successful human being would ever consider, let alone do, such a mad thing.

JUDAH: If we're putting all our cards on the table, you must admit there's something to that, isn't there?

ISRAEL: What do you mean?

JUDAH: That living in Israel means opting for a lower quality of life.

ISRAEL: What do you mean by quality of life?

JUDAH: Your income, your home, your car, the comforts you can afford, the things you can buy when you want them.

ISRAEL: It's certainly true that I can't match you in that respect. But are such things the only or even the most important ingredients of the good life? Don't get me wrong. I'd be the last to look down on a big car, a fancy house, a good meal, or a five-star hotel. Such things no doubt make life more pleasant: But as a relish, not as the main course or as a substitute for something more substantial—like the experience of building a country. Of actually owning the home you live in. Of living in a society that still judges you by your character and talents rather than by how much money you've got in the bank.

I'm getting carried away with myself, though. What matters is how *you* see it, and *you* see life in terms of money and its uses. That's why anyone exchanging more of these for less seems bizarre to you.

JUDAH: And to you, too.

ISRAEL: I beg your pardon?

JUDAH: Why don't you try sometime going to the aliyah desk of a Jewish Agency office and announcing that you want to settle in Israel? As soon as you've opened your mouth you'll get an odd look from the man behind the desk. You can see what he's thinking: something, no doubt, will turn out to be the matter with you.

Next, he hands you a pile of forms full of questions. Have you ever had psychiatric treatment? Do you take or have you ever taken drugs? Are you a homosexual? And if you pass every test, you still can't count on acceptance. Like a certain man I knew who seemed ideal. An engineer in his middle thirties with a lovely wife who was a teacher and two lovely children. What more could you ask for? The problem was that there was a third child, a seven-year-old who had been adopted. Not that the Jewish Agency is against adoption. But the boy was a dark-skinned Vietnamese, one of those keepsakes left behind in Vietnam by black American soldiers. The would-be immigrant wanted to join a moshav, a farming cooperative. His application was circulated from one moshav to another and turned down by every one. None said why. Just that the family seemed "problematic." The man remained in the United States. Today he's a voluntary adviser to several Palestinian organizations. So what's all this talk about you wanting immigrants?

ISRAEL: All that proves is that sometimes I can be as insensitive and prejudiced as the next man.

JUDAH: One of your aliyah officials told me that once he decided to send a form to the main office in Jerusalem in the name of an elderly applicant who was married to a black woman, had no profession, and suffered from a speech defect. "Are you crazy?" came the immediate answer. The official had, of course, given an exact description of Moses.

And even if you come through with flying colors and actually arrive in Israel, you're hardly met with a wave of enthusiasm, to put it mildly. I knew a Jew who was really the perfect immigrant. A man in his early forties with a Jewish wife and two children of the right color. He had worked all his life in an American Jewish organization in which he had risen to be vice president. Everyone knew him. Your leaders never missed a chance to drop in on him whenever they were in New York. One day he decided to move to Israel. His Israeli friends, when told of his decision, did not seem particularly elated. It was a great thing to do, they told him, but took a lot of courage—the word "courage" was repeated many times—and he should think it over carefully and not act impulsively.

The man's mind was made up, however, and he soon arrived with his family and belongings in the Promised Land. His first stop was the office of a tired-looking petty official in the Department of Immigration. The new immigrant told him that he would like to live in the Tel Aviv area. That was his first mistake. Immigrants are not expected to choose where they are going to live. Without bothering to swallow the salami sandwich he was chewing, the official declared that the Tel Aviv area had no available apartments. The new immigrant, he announced, would live in Beersheba.

As politely as possible, our immigrant reiterated that he wanted to live near Tel Aviv.

"I'm sorry, but that's out of the question. You'll have to take Beersheba."

When the immigrant patiently explained that he already had work in Tel Aviv, the official could not believe his ears. "If you don't like it, go find help somewhere else," he told him, adding when the man had left to his friend, Official 2: "Just look at them! They think we owe them the world."

Of course, our immigrant had heard about the importance of personal connections in Israel, but he wanted to do things on the level. In the end, though, he couldn't take it anymore. When in Rome, do as the Romans. And so he phoned a few of the politicians who used to invite him to their homes whenever he visited Israel. All were too busy to see him. Perhaps next week. Or the week after that. Until finally he caught on. They didn't need him anymore. He had sawed off the branch he had been sitting on with his own hands. No longer could he take them out for dinner to an expensive restaurant in New York on his vice president's expense account. No longer could he schedule them a whirlwind tour of America paid for by the Jewish people.

It took him a while, but in the end he realized it was hopeless. He had gone from being a vice president to being a pesky immigrant. And the leaders of Israel had no time for pesky immigrants. They were too busy hosting and being hosted by the vice presidents who were still on the job.

Within a few months our immigrant returned to America. He still visits Israel twice a year. On each visit he has a long audience with some of your senior politicians.

So why in the world should it surprise you that I think it takes an imbecile to immigrate to Israel?

Well, why don't you say something?

ISRAEL: Because you're right. And because your story proves not only that I can be stupid, but that you haven't understood a word I've said. We're back to our vicious circle again. Why do you think I'm so suspicious of immigrants from America? Because most of them really are—what's a tactful way of putting it—"problematic." When do you ask me to help one of them? "Listen, do me a favor. My wife's cousin—it seems he's into drugs. His parents think that maybe in Israel, if he went to a kibbutz or someplace, he might get over it. Be a pal and find a place for him, will you?" Or: "Look, my wife's sister, her husband just left her. She has two pretty big kids and is in a depression. My wife says she has to find herself a man and thinks that maybe in Israel she can start a new life. Do you think you could place her in an absorption center?"

You've made me your human dumping grounds.

Believe me, we have enough problems without your case loads. You say you don't come to live in Israel because I reject you when the truth is that I reject you because you only come if you're abnormal.

156

JUDAH: What was abnormal about that vice president? Is that part of your vicious circle, too?

ISRAEL: Fine—suppose that in this case I agree with you that it's my fault, that I'm insensitive, that I'm thoughtless, that I'm arrogant and inconsiderate—you know what I say to you? Come, help me to change things, that's what. If that's the way I am, it must have a lot to do with the difficulties I face, with the physical insecurity I've had to live with since birth, with my being so small. I'm sure that if I were taller, broader, stronger, more efficient, more secure, most of my bad qualities would disappear.

You find it easier, however, to keep on revolving in the vicious circle: You won't come because of my negative qualities, which I have because you're not here.

JUDAH: There's something humanly warped about your whole theory. First come to live in Israel, you say, and that will make it a country I'll want to live in. I think your vicious circle starts and ends in the wrong place. If you want people to leave one country for another, you first have to convince them that they'll like it, that they're exchanging their old lives for better ones.

ISRAEL: I'll never be able to give you bigger houses, fancier cars, higher incomes . . .

JUDAH: That's not what I'm talking about.

ISRAEL: Then what are you talking about?

JUDAH: Take a look at yourself in the mirror. What do you see? A warrior. Nearly all your time is spent fighting the Arabs and fighting with yourself. The Peace-firsters against the Land-firsters. The Sabbath-observers against the non-

157

Sabbath-observers. Everything turns into a war with you, which you fight at the top of your voice, frantically hitting below the belt. You export arms instead of culture. You create generals instead of books. I had hoped you would build a new society. Cleaner. More cultured. More spiritual. More just.

ISRAEL: A light unto the Gentiles.

JUDAH: I would settle for the Jews.

ISRAEL: And you're disappointed that that's not what I am. I've failed you yet another time. You wanted me to establish a state, to absorb a million homeless immigrants, to defend myself against hundreds of millions of Arabs— and in the same breath to create a new culture and a great literature. You expected me to surrender most of my earnings in taxes to pay for an army to protect this country—for you as well as for me—and also to establish a highly civilized and urbane style of life.

Well, if that's what you expected, let me tell you in plain words that it's too much for me. Establishing a state and fighting for survival while constructing a model culture and society at the same time is too tall an order. It's more than I'm capable of. I can't do all that and take in needy immigrants and be a spiritual beacon of light to you. Sorry, but I can't do it by myself.

You want a beacon? Then come here and help me make it. You want me to look nicer? Then come and share the load with me. Maybe then I'll have time to worry about my appearance and to be the beacon that I'd like me to be as much as you would, because I too want to live in a country that is concerned with creativity and not just brute survival. That's something I'd like to be for my own sake, not just to be a light for you.

Shall I tell you something, though? Nevertheless, in spite of all I've said, if I knew that being a beacon would be enough to bring you here, I would make every effort to be one. As hard as that would be. Despite all the pressures on me. Even though it's unfair of you to demand it of me. I would do my best nonetheless. I would restructure my priorities. For example: I would cut back on defense spending in order to free more financial and human resources for education and culture. And I would do this without feeling that I was taking too great a risk, because your presence in Israel would be the best defense I could buy!

Why, then, don't I make the effort? Because I know that you won't come anyway. And then I'll be left with the beacon, but without adequate defense. That's a luxury I can't afford. Did I say beacon? I could light a bonfire that would be seen from one end of the world to the other— you still wouldn't come! Your record speaks for itself. After all, there was a time when you did consider me the bright light that you speak of. Remember? It was right after the Six Day War. You loved and admired me along with the rest of the world; you thought me infallible and unable to do wrong. I was the darling of the West, a shining light in a dark world.

True, you took a step in my direction in those days. Something did give a little. Who among you didn't want to visit Israel then and rub elbows with the heroes who vanquished three Arab armies in six days? Who didn't want to feel somehow part of us? We especially attracted your young people, whose imaginations were fired by the war and its aftermath. Some said they were coming for good, others as volunteers for a while. Adults, too, came in greater numbers than before, not a few with the express intention of "giving it a try."

After a few months, not much was left of all the enthusiasm. Not much was left of the hundreds of thousands of visitors either. At most a few thousand stayed.

So you see, the issue isn't a real one. You won't come no matter how much light I give off. Because I still won't be able to give you a big car, a big house, and the Bahamas and Hawaii, together with a fat bank account, an army you don't have to serve in, and a familiar style of life. You can talk all you want about culture, education, civility, but what you really mean is that you don't want to leave the fleshpots.

JUDAH: That's only human.

ISRAEL: Of course it is. but why not say so! Why make it seem that it's my fault? I refuse to hold myself responsible for the fact that you don't come to live with me. You're trying to have your cake and eat it too. Both to stay in America and to blame it on me, when your staying there is a main reason that I am what I am.

SELECTIVE FREEDOM OF CHOICE

JUDAH: I don't think it's fair to berate me for not settling in Israel when so many Israelis are emigrating to America. I see them everywhere. There are more and more of them all the time.

ISRAEL: Dreadful, isn't it? I'm sure it must break your heart. And what are you doing about it? You're helping them to emigrate. You give them jobs in your organizations and institutions—the same organizations and institutions that are financed with money raised for me, my money. It's hard to find an American Jewish organization today that doesn't have at least one Israeli émigré working for it. You find them even at the highest levels.

JUDAH: Do you want me to punish them? *You* can't keep them in Israel, yet you ask me to do it for you by ostracizing them in America! I'm very sorry, but I believe in the human right to live wherever one wants.

ISRAEL: Ah, yes, your renowned right. As if anyone were challenging it. As if you didn't understand that the other side of the coin is the right not to exercise that right. Can't you see the absurdity in giving Israeli émigrés jobs in organizations that are supposed to work for Israel? Don't you realize that it's like hiring a hijacker to be a security agent with El Al?

Recently you've even decided to let Israeli émigrés join your Jewish federations. Your stated reason? If you don't do what you can to befriend them, they may be lost to the Jewish community. Which translates as: You want them for their money. Not belonging to the federation and the community means being out of the reach of the money machine. You want them in organized fashion, with files and income estimates and pledge assessments. The fact that they were once Israelis, in your opinion, is no reason to give them a Jewish tax exemption. As usual with you, the short-term benefits take precedence. You can't and don't want to think ahead. You don't want to be told, you don't want to know that you're legitimizing emigration from Israel. I'm not saying you have to ostracize the émigrés. All that I'm saying is that there's no reason to embrace them.

Did I say no reason? That was a slip of the tongue. It's the same reason that made you encourage Soviet Jews to go to America, that made you prefer them to go there—the very same . . .

JUDAH: Just a minute. Not so fast! Soviet Jews are a different story. To begin with, most of them are now coming directly to you, so that the problem has been solved.

ISRAEL: It took a long struggle to arrive at that, and even today you're not reconciled to it. Many of you are still fighting for more visas for Soviet Jews. I wouldn't bet against your finding a way of at least partially turning the clock back.

JUDAH: You're certainly right that I view aid to Soviet Jewry as a sacred cause. One of the most basic fundamentals in the Jewish heritage is that all Jews are responsible for each other. When a Jew is in trouble, it's my duty to help him. First let's get him out of an anti-Semitic Russia. We can deal with the issues of where he'll live later.

ISRAEL: How noble of you! And as usual, it's I who end up paying for your nobility. Because what did you do by aiding Russians to go to America? You in effect encouraged them not to come to Israel. For years your representatives were active in the transit camps for Soviet Jews near Rome, promising them that if only they went to America you would help them financially to get settled and find housing. During that period 95 percent of the Jews leaving Russia did just that. Nearly all of them! Why? Why did you do it?

JUDAH: Because I honestly think that everyone has the right to live where he pleases.

ISRAEL: Yes, I believe I've heard that before. Freedom of choice for Soviet Jews . . . who was just talking about it? Ah, yes. Permit me to quote: "I'm against Jews immigrating to Israel. But I am against the United States and other Western countries limiting Soviet Jewish immigration to them. I think that every man should be allowed to live where he pleases. It's wrong to make Jews go to Israel. They must be given a free choice." Do you know who said that?

JUDAH: I'm afraid you'll have to enlighten me.

ISRAEL: Feisal el-Husseini, the PLO's chief representative in the occupied territories, as interviewed in the Israeli newspaper *Yediot Ahoronot*.* Odd, isn't it?

JUDAH: What's so odd about it?

ISRAEL: That whoever doesn't want Soviet Jews to come to Israel talks about freedom of choice. Suddenly both you and the PLO have become such democrats! Unlike you, I really do believe in freedom of choice—but not on a selective basis. That's why it would never occur to me to force Soviet Jews to live in Israel or anywhere else. If a Jew from Russia wants to live in America, let him go right

---

* The interview, conducted by Dan Shilon, appeared on January 26, 1990.

ahead. But since when does that mean you have to help him to do it?

JUDAH: My Jewish tradition obligates me to help Jewish refugees who are fleeing distress.

ISRAEL: You still can't stop mouthing clichés! Those people weren't refugees and they weren't in distress. Do you know what a refugee is? It's someone who has nowhere to go, because no country will take him in. We're no longer living in the first half of this century when that was the case with Jews. Now there's an Israel. And I've always been prepared to take in every Soviet Jew. I'm eager to take them in. I'm willing to make great personal sacrifices to do it. Those of them who chose America, therefore, were not refugees. They were not really emigrating to you from Russia, they were emigrating to you from Israel. Do you consider Israel a country in which Jews are in distress?

JUDAH: But those Soviet Jews did not want to come to Israel. Suppose I had stopped helping them: Wouldn't the knowledge that they were coming to you against their will have upset you?

ISRAEL: Upset me? Beggars can't be choosers.

JUDAH: But that puts me in a very tight spot.

ISRAEL: You didn't feel you were in such a tight spot when it came to Ethiopian Jews. Or to Moroccan Jews before them. I didn't hear you talking about freedom of choice or helping Jews in distress then. Then you were only too happy to give me money to take them off your hands. Why didn't you give them the same right of freedom of choice?

JUDAH: To the best of my memory, there was no problem then because they wanted to go to Israel.

ISRAEL: What makes you so sure? Did you ask them? Did you tell them that if they went to America they would be helped no less than in Israel, as you tell Soviet Jews today? No, you did no such thing. You made it clear to them that if they wanted out of Moroco or Ethiopia, there was only one way: that leading to Israel.

So why don't we put your selective freedoms aside and return to hard reality?

You have a problem. A real one. You live in America. And you want to go on living in America. The larger the American Jewish community is, the safer and more comfortable your life there will be. A smaller community means less security. Fewer members. Fewer institutions. Fewer facilities. Less money. In a word, it's bad news.

JUDAH: It's bad news for you, too. The fewer my numbers, the less able I will be to give you the financial and political support that you get from me today. I already know what you think of my money. I can't imagine, though, that you think the same way about the $3 billion that you get every year from Washington. And I can't believe that you don't take seriously the influence I have on your getting that aid and on U.S. policy in the Middle East and toward Israel.

ISRAEL: I certainly take it more seriously than you take me, because I'm beginning to think you haven't heard a word I've said. Do you mean to tell me you still don't get the principle of the vicious circle?

Why do I need your political support? Because I'm small and weak. Because I'm in a state of war. Give me 6 million more Jews—give me 2 million!—and I won't need your political support. I'll be strong in and of myself, without recourse to others. I won't need financial support of any kind, because I'll probably be at peace, and in any case, I'll have created—together with you!—a well-run society and economy. Together we can build a country that any other country will want to support not because its president needs Jewish votes, but because we are worth supporting. That's always a healthier basis to do business on.

And yet there's no budging you: You won't come, you say, because you want to give me the support I need in America when the only reason I need that support is because you haven't come. A single big, strong Jewish community in Israel is far better for me than many big, strong Jewish communities in the United States. But your main concern is the survival of American Jewry—and the more American Jews disappear into the maws of Christian America, the more Jews you need to import from abroad.

That's why you want Soviet Jews.

That's why you want Israeli émigrés.

That's why you don't want American immigration to Israel.

Those are the real reasons. All the rest—freedom of choice, freedom of movement, and all the other nice slogans—is just a smoke screen.

JUDAH: If my memory serves me right, you said a while back that what I really wanted was to assimilate. Now you're telling me that what I really want is to strengten the Jewish community and the Jew in myself.

ISRAEL: I said that you were beginning to make your peace

with assimilation. That unconsciously you were beginning to accept it and to stop viewing it negatively. But the process is still embryonic. Until it runs its full course years will pass in which you will continue to be a split soul. You'll still be loathe to surrender your communal identity but neither will you be willing to make any sacrifices to maintain it. What, then, is the solution? To bring fresh Jews who will fill the vacuum you have created.

JUDAH: Do you really believe that if I cut off aid to Soviet Jews, stop being nice to Israeli émigrés, and change my attitude toward would-be immigrants to Israel, the situation is going to change?

ISRAEL: What better example is there than Soviet Jews? When they flew to transit camps in Austria or Italy and you offered to help them, they went to America. Now that they are being flown directly to Israel and your offer no longer exists, they are staying here with me.

JUDAH: Then there's no longer any problem.

ISRAEL: You'd like that, wouldn't you?

JUDAH: I'd like what?

ISRAEL: For me to take the Jews of Russia and leave you alone in peace. There are just three things wrong with that. I've already mentioned the first—the fact that, at least in the short and medium term, absorbing so many Jews coming without means from an economically uncompetitive society is a heavy burden that I'm not sure how to cope with.

Secondly, those Jews are not enough. Even if the most optimistic estimates of their numbers prove true, they will still not dramatically change the demographic balance between us and the Arabs or decrease our vulnerability.

But the third reason is the most important. Because I'm not talking just about my own good, my friend, I'm talking about yours, too. And I'm convinced that your settling in Israel is as vital for your survival as it is for mine. That's something that Soviet Jewish immigration has nothing to do with.

JUDAH: I greatly appreciate your concern, but why don't you leave my own problems up to me?

ISRAEL: Believe me, I'd love to. I'm not looking for more problems. But I can't afford to leave it up to you, because your surviving is my problem as much as yours. You have the biggest reserve of Jews in the world, and it's one that we're all dependent on.

Soviet Jewish immigration is of great importance. It does not, however, change the basic situation.

JUDAH: What can change it?

ISRAEL: Breaking out of the vicious circle.

JUDAH: How is that going to be done?

ISRAEL: By your coming to Israel. Because if you're here, I won't need you there. Because if you begin coming, I'll grow much bigger and stronger, and then you'll keep on coming. And then I really can be a beacon of light—to the Jews of Israel and to the Jews outside of it. That's when Israelis will stop leaving and Jews from abroad will start coming. They won't come because non-Jews are making them, but because, for the first time in the history of Zionism, it's a place they really want to live in.

The key to breaking out of the vicious circle, I'm sorry to say, is in your hands.

JUDAH: Why be sorry?

ISRAEL: Because I'm sure you'll never use it.

A COZY JEWISH CLUB

JUDAH: What makes you so sure that I won't break the vicious circle?

ISRAEL: For two reasons. The first is that no one wants you to.

JUDAH: You certainly seem to want me to.

ISRAEL: But my political leaders don't.

JUDAH: Your leaders don't want me to come to Israel? Is that what you're saying?

ISRAEL: Not exactly. Of course they would like you to come. Very much so. It's just that they're resigned to your not doing it and aren't prepared to have it out with you. They don't want to annoy you, because just like your leaders, they're concerned first and foremost with their own private welfare. They would prefer you gave philanthropy rather than invest because part of your contribution goes to their political parties. The Jewish Agency employs a legion of bureaucrats of whom many are political appointees, and what politician wants to hurt his ward heelers in their pockets? And so they tell themselves that it's hopeless, that you'll never come in any case, and that they might as well accept it and make the best of it.

And make the best of it they do. You're an expert at

stroking their egos. Here in Israel they have to take criticism, to win supporters and votes. In America all they hear is praise. The minute they open their mouths you start to cheer as though they had said something earthshaking. Before they finish speaking you're on your feet with a standing ovation, even though you've heard it a dozen times before. "Congratulations," you tell them, slapping them on the back, "that was a great speech, a great speech."

You not only butter them up, you give them the time of their lives. You show them America—and in style. The wife, of course, is left behind in New York so that she can spend their expense accounts in Bloomingdales—they themselves won't be needing them, because you pick up all their tabs. You have a man waiting for them in every city to chauffeur them about, register them in the best hotels, wine them, dine them, and take them out on the town. Not a penny of it comes out of their own pockets, in which, like true aristocrats, they need only keep their handkerchiefs. Naturally, when they return to Israel, they can't stop marveling over how cheap everything in America is. And if they're famous enough, they'll go home with several thousands, perhaps even several tens of thousands, of dollars.

Let me read to you from an old circular of the Harry Walker Lecture Bureau in New York: "We are bringing Abba Eban, former prime minister Yitzchak Rabin, and former U.N. ambassador Ya'akov Herzog back to the United States. Ambassador Eban's schedule is already full. Rabin and Herzog are available for $3,500 plus expenses. Please call soon to make your reservations."

This letter went out in 1978. You mustn't imagine that I cite it to make you think that our leaders can be had cheaply. They're no longer available at the old price. What, you ask, are they being paid all that money for? Is it to speak about the miracle cure they've discovered for cancer? About their literary or artistic careers? No, it's to talk about me! Me and my problems. The problems they're supposed to solve, though they make a better lecture topic unsolved, to say nothing of a more profitable one.

They love every minute of it: the getting-to-know-you, the "Hi, Steven" and "Hey there, Milton," the backslapping, the cocktail parties, the hobnobbing with the celebrities whom you invite to meet them, the weekends in your summer home. And they're not so choosy about whom they befriend anymore. Once, if you were an Israeli émigré, they kept you at arm's length. Then a few years passed and they were willing to meet you—secretly. Then a few more years went by and they met you openly but squirmed a bit. Now there's no longer any problem. Ex-Israeli Meshulam Riklis hosts Ariel Sharon, Ilana Gur entertains Shimon Peres. In fact, the Sharons and Pereses can't wait for an invitation. They're willing to sell themselves and their self-respect—me and my self-respect—in return for a steak dinner and a chance to mix with high society.

And in order to keep these juicy tidbits coming their way—the free trips, the entertainment, the expense accounts, the lecturers' fees, the socializing with your upper crust—they'll tell you whatever you want to hear. Only a party-pooper would refuse to reassure you how vital your contribution is, and to tell you you're a partner in the building of Israel, and to promise you that the Jewish people need you in America. And of course, mum's the word on aliyah. They've learned their lesson from Ben-Gurion. *He* tried telling you in no uncertain terms that a Zionist is a Jew who decides to live in Israel, period—and he was far from popular with you because of it. Today no one would dream of saying such a thing. We had hopes for Menachem Begin when he became prime minister, but he too preferred your warm bosom and loud applause to a direct confrontation.

And so nowadays everything goes smoothly. Our leader arrives in New York and invites your leaders for breakfast (or for lunch or dinner—as long as there's food on the table) in his suite at the Pierre or the Waldorf or the Regency. Over the appetizer he tells them about The Situation. Over the entrée they tell him what they think about The Situation. Over dessert it's agreed that something has to be done about The Situation. So much for that: Our leader has earned his trip. Now coffee and brandy are served and it's time for the fun part: How is the wife? How are the kids? Won't you spend the weekend at my summer place? I know a new French restaurant on the East Side that's a must; whatever you do, don't miss *Phantom of the Opera.*

Time for a little business, too. Over the years a class of well situated Israelis, usually lawyers who have gone into politics, have used this opportunity to land some fat clients who have made them rich.

It's an exclusive, cozy little club whose members get along just fine and will continue to do so as long as they observe the house rules. And because no one has any interest in breaking these rules, they will go on being observed.

This is the conspiracy of silence and deceit that I have spoken of. You'll tell me what I want to hear, I'll tell you what you want to hear, the two of us will do everything to keep the truth from rearing its ugly head—and now please pass the champagne!

MAC THE JEW

The second reason I'm convinced that we won't break out of the vicious circle is that you and your leadership are the way Jews always have been. Throughout the history of Zionism the land of Israel has never been freely chosen by more than a small minority. Most of the Jewish people have preferred and continue to prefer other places.

As an ideology, Zionism is a Jewish creation. As something to put into practice, however, it is largely the doing of Gentiles.

How many Jews ever came to Palestine of their own free will, because of their conviction that it was the only place for a Jew to live and build his home? No more than a handful of eccentric ideologues. The great majority of Jews who wound up here do so because their non-Jewish neighbors made their lives intolerable and there was nowhere else for them to go.

The first wave of Zionist immigration to Palestine, which took place roughly one hundred years ago (1882–1904), was in the main a reaction to anti-Jewish pogroms and expulsions in Russia. Several thousand more Jews arrived in those years from Yemen, which also had a brutally anti-Jewish regime. At the beginning of this period, the entire Jewish population of Palestine was 26,000. By the end of it, it had reached 55,000.

A new series of pogroms, starting with the bloody 1903 massacre in Kishinev that saw dozens of Jews murdered, hundreds wounded, and wholesale destruction and looting of property, set off a second wave of Zionist emigration. Thirty thousand more Jews came to Palestine before the outbreak of the First World War, although most of them subsequently left for elsewhere. (According to Ben-Gurion, 90 percent of the Second Aliyah reemigrated. Other estimates are lower, but all agree that a majority did not remain.)

During the Third Aliyah (1919–23), 35,000 strong came, largely from the Soviet Union in the wake of the Bolshevik Revolution and the massacres of Jews by the White Army during the Civil War. It was followed by the mostly Polish Fourth Aliyah (1924–28), whose members escaped growing political and commercial anti-Semitism aimed largely at Jewish professionals and businessmen. Most of its immigrants were petty merchants (rather than pioneers) who opened small businesses and shops here. They, too, did not stay long. Of the 19,000 who arrived in the country, 14,000 left during the economic crisis of 1926.

With the Fifth Aliyah began the flight from Nazi-dominated Europe. Its main element, culturally if not numerically, was composed of Jews from Germany. In 1934–35, the year of Hitler's takeover, 65,000 European Jews arrived in Palestine, an unprecedented number at the time.

Finally, there was the great exodus from Europe after World War II. The Nazi horror had left hundreds of thousands of homeless survivors. Did they opt en masse for Palestine in order to establish a Jewish national home there? Had they learned the lesson of the Holocaust? Only a minority actually wished to go to Palestine. Most preferred other countries but had no choice, because none would take them in. Many (such as Elie Wiesel himself) left the new state of Israel as soon as they found an alternative.

Luckily for us and for Zionism, the alternatives were few and far between. Can you imagine what would have happened had the countries of the world opened their gates wide to Jews in those years? Most Jews would have flowed through those gates, which was exactly what the Western world was afraid of—to the point that it supported the establishment of a Jewish state so that Jewish refugees would have somewhere to go. The theories of Herzl, Sokolov, Weizmann, and other Zionist thinkers would have remained no more than theories were it not for the barbarism that drove the Jews out of Europe and the refusal of the Western democracies to grant them asylum.

If all this smacks too much of ancient history, we can look at some more recent examples. Take the Jews of Iran when they fled Khomeini after the fall of the Shah; the Jews of Russia escaping from Communist totalitarianism when there was somewhere beside Israel to take them in; the Jews of South Africa running away from an impending black-white civil war. Where did they all go? Very few came to me. Most went to you, to the West. Do you understand the terrible significance of all this? I'm talking about people who were already on the run, who were forced to leave jobs and friends and adapt themselves to a new way of thinking. And even then they did not come to Israel.

JUDAH: Perhaps it's a matter of education—that is, of not enough education of a Jewish and Zionist nature.

ISRAEL: I have two problems with that. The first is that, no matter how hard it tries, I'm not at all sure that contemporary Judaism has the intellectual means to make its case. Perhaps it's no longer possible to raise a Jew today with the realization that it's important and worthwhile to stay Jewish.

More serious, though, is the fact that education is not the answer in any case. If it were, we should be able to see its results, whereas what do we actually see? Iranian Jewry received a comprehensive traditional education and still did not come to Israel when it left Iran. The Jews of South Africa are given an excellent Jewish and Zionist education. They're emigrating from South Africa, but not for Israel. Orthodox Jews from all over the world are not coming to Israel in any great numbers either.

JUDAH: Well, if education won't help, and the anti-Semites won't do their bit either, what will happen?

ISRAEL: What will happen is that Zionism, that crazy, wonderful Jewish dream, will pass away. It's already on the verge of bankruptcy.

JUDAH: How can you say that? After all, Israel exists.

ISRAEL: Zionism's aim was for the Jewish state to be the national home of the Jewish people. That hasn't happened. Israel is the home of a minority of that people. And it's a tired minority. It can't and doesn't want to carry the burden by itself any longer.

JUDAH: It infuriates me to hear you talk like that. Israel can be whatever you will it to be.

ISRAEL: You don't say! It's all up to me, eh? There are no situations or circumstances that might be beyond my control? As if we Jews haven't lost our independence more than once in the past despite our will to maintain it!

Still, it is true that much does depend on our will—and our will, I'm sorry to say, is not what it used to be. We're burned out. We're exhausted. I talk with my friends. All were born in this country. All hold important jobs. All have good incomes. And nearly all are ready to leave Israel. I say "nearly all" just to be on the safe side, not because I actually know of any exceptions. Offer them a good, well-paying job in America and they'll start packing immediately. Some of them will say that it's only for a few years, until they can salt away a little nest egg. Some will say that it's just to continue their studies. But they won't come back. They hardly ever do. Many of us already have children living abroad, most of them in America. They don't intend to return either. Nearly all of us—the "nearly" is again a formality—have learned to accept that. "Have learned"? "Are happy" might be more accurate.

JUDAH: What happened to that special quality of Israeli life you spoke about before, to the experience of building a country?

ISRAEL: There's no experience, not even the most powerful, that doesn't get eroded when the struggle to maintain it seems endless.

JUDAH: What are you trying to tell me? That Israel is something you've given up on?

ISRAEL: I'm trying to tell you that I'm tired. I've had enough of being the Jewish Mac.

JUDAH: What's a Jewish Mac?

ISRAEL: You should know, because it's a creation of yours. It's the man—usually a non-Jew, usually old, usually alone in life, always a sad case—whom you hire to guard your summer camps in the winter. Each summer you bring your children to camp and they have a wonderful time. When the summer is over, they get on buses and go home. As they pass through the front gate they wave to poor old Mac, whom they won't see again till next summer.

I don't want to be your Jewish Mac anymore.

You want a Jewish state? Then please be so kind as to stand guard over it yourself. I've been doing it for dozens of years. Now it's your turn. Let's switch lives. You come here, serve in the army, worry about the *Intifada,* deal with the Orthodox, and shell out 50 percent of your income taxes, and I'll live in America, send you money, and visit you now and then, and criticize. Didn't you say we were partners? Then it seems to me a fair offer. I've given this project called Israel over forty years of my life. Why don't you give forty years of yours now, and I'll support you financially and politically. You can tell me what a crucial role I play in America, and I'll tell you how wonderful it is that you live in Israel.

Because I just can't take it anymore.

Epilogue

My conversation with Elie Wiesel touched on only a few of the issues that have been raised in this dialogue. But it was wide-ranging enough for Wiesel to have said, "I never knew that Israelis felt like that about us. What you say is very serious, even if I don't agree with all of it. Instead of arguing with you, though, I'd like to do something practical. What I suggest is this. You pick five prominent youing Israelis, leading figures in various fields of life, I'll pick five young American Jews, and we'll arrange to meet somewhere—let's say, in Geneva—for a marathon of several days in which we'll discuss the issues you raised. If at the end we reach the conclusion that you're right, we'll issue a manifesto to the Jews of America, calling on them to settle in Israel. I'll contact you to set a time and place for our meeting. What do you say to that?"

"I say that all you're doing is sending it back to committee."

"What does that mean?"

"It means that once we say good-bye I'll never hear from you again."

"What makes you say that?"

"The fact that such a disscusion goes against your interests. You want to go on living in the United States. You like it there. You're a prominent intellectual, you're a welcome guest in the homes of presidents and tycoons, you get paid handsome fees for your lectures. What you're proposing could only spoil the nice life you have. Suppose, perish the thought, that we actually ended with a call to settle in Israel—what would you do then? You would be expected to go first, which is the last thing in the world you want to do."

181

"How can you say that? You don't even know me."

"I don't have to know you. I know the likes of you. But I'll give you the chance to prove me wrong—and I'll put my money where my mouth is. Let's make a little wager. If I do hear from you, I'll give you a thousand dollars. It doesn't matter what you write. It can even be, "Dear Matti, I tried but couldn't swing it." That wins a thousand dollars, too. Fair enough?"

"There's no need for bets. Within a month you'll receive a letter from me with the names of the five people I've chosen to participate in the discussion."

We said good-bye.

I waited three months. Then I sent the following letter:

"Dear Elie Wiesel,

Just as I predicted in Jerusalem, I still haven't heard form you. This doesn't surprise me, but in order to be sporting I'm willing to give you another chance to prove I was wrong about you. I'll double the ante: write me a single word and I'll send you two thousand dollars. This time too, though, I predict that I'll never hear from you.

That was some five years ago.

I kept my two thousand dollars, and Elie Wiesel went on living in America. Last Holocaust Memorial Day we saw him on television discussing the Holocaust—which, he said, must never happen again.

What is Elie Wiesel doing to help assure that it never happens again? He is telling American Jews about the vital role they have to play in America and making speeches.

For this he was awarded the Nobel Peace Prize. Shortly after he received this prize, in January 1991, the Gulf War broke out. Israel was bombed almost daily by Scud missiles launched from Iraq. An atmosphere of fear and anxiety gripped the country, as normal life nearly drew to a standstill. Families left their homes to seek shelter in places far from Tel Aviv, which was the main target of the bombing. People spent most of their time in sealed rooms to provide protection against gas attacks and other chemical weapons. The wail of the sirens became the hallmark of life in those days. Members of the presidents Conference came to Israel for forty-eight hours to show their solidarity. There were other Jews who came, among them Elie Wiesel. The *Hadashot* newspaper reported on his visit (February 2, 1991):

> Wiesel arrived in Israel on January 15, spent a day here, was interviewed on TV and in the press, and left. The whole affair, which looked like a PR stunt, aroused the anger of several literary figures who are in touch with him, one of whom said to me last week: "Write that Wiesel should not have been given the Nobel Prize but rather an Oscar for his brilliant acting performance." I was going to write that, but in the meantime, towards the end of last week, Wiesel came back to Israel, and thus seemingly gave the lie to all the rumors about him. In a phone conversation he said that this time he had come "for a long time, until the war is over," and described to me how on Wednesday, he had been sitting in a sealed room, with small children. "It's an indescribably shocking sight," he said, "to think of such small children wearing gas masks against chemical weapons made by the Germans."
>
> I looked for Wiesel again three days later. I tried the hotel, where I was told he had gone to Tel Aviv, a really heroic act, and had left a phone number. I tried to reach Wiesel late in the evening, but there was no reply from that number. I tried the next day, and a woman answered.

"No," she said, "Professor Wiesel isn't here at the moment." She didn't know when he would return but she could take a message for him. "It's quite urgent," I said. "Professor Wiesel is in Paris," she said, "he was called there urgently on Saturday. He'll return to Israel, but I don't know when. Maybe this week, maybe next week. He'll inform me." And "Who are you?" I asked. "Where did I call? Are you his friend?" "No," she replied, "you called Bank Discount; you're talking to Yosef Chichanover's secretary. Yosef Chichanover* is a friend of Professor Wiesel's, and he asked me, at Wiesel's request, to take messages for Wiesel."

As I was writing these words, my son came home on leave from the army. I hadn't seen him in three weeks. He said hello, slipped off his knapsack, put his rifle down on the bed, lay down in bed himself, and went to sleep for twenty-six hours. He was too exhausted to even get up to eat.

My son is an officer in a combat unit. He's fought terrorists in Lebanon and chased rock throwers on the West Bank.

To keep it from happening again.

Elie Wiesel came, he saw, and he fled.

He was awarded the Nobel Prize for being a proud Jew constantly fighting for his people—wherever they are.

The prize awarded me was my son's coming home safely.

And that, in a nutshell, is the vicious circle.

---

* Chairman of the bank.

Acknowledgments

After many transatlantic telephone conversations and several meetings in New York, I knew I was blessed with the fulfilment of every author's wish: a good editor. In his quiet and intelligent manner, Adam Bellow weeded out some rough spots, clarified concepts, helped me to develop some ideas that had previously seemed to lead nowhere. And perhaps most important of all, he knew how to give me what an author needs more that anything else: the feeling that an editor believes in his book.

But before the book got to the stage of editing, before the ideas became a finished book, there was Nili, now my wife, always my friend. The encounter between my ideas and her investigative intelligence enriched the writing of this book throughout—just as the idea of writing it in the form of a dialogue was hers.